High Shelf

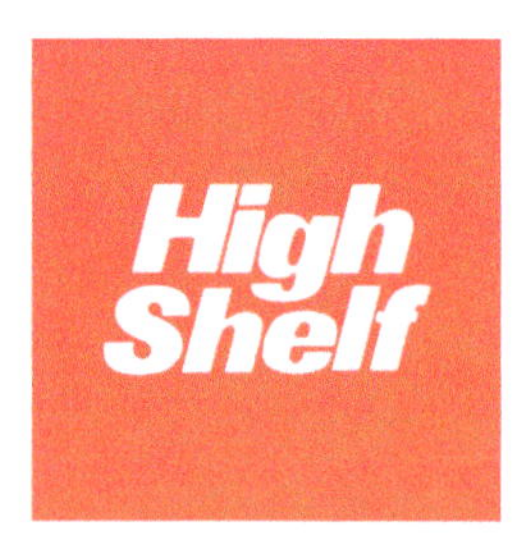

High Shelf XIV, January 2020
Portland, Oregon.
Copyright 2020, High Shelf Press

ISBN: 978-1-7342842-4-9

Cover Image by Ami J. Sanghvi
Design and Layout by C. M. Tollefson
Edited by David Seung & C. M. Tollefson

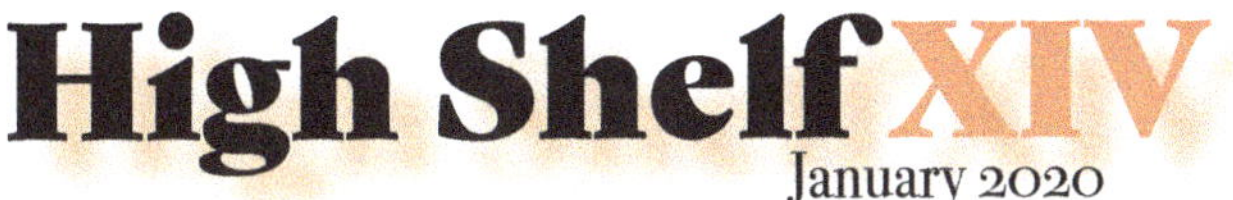

High Shelf XIV

January 2020

"... Call the behavior
pseudo-copulation
call the flower
prostitute
A frenzy of intercourse
ensures pollination.. "
Valyntina Grenier

"We enter the cemetery to touch
the illegible names on stones,

quiet and damp to our skin
as cellars, even now, when

the brittle August grass

breaks under us like cereal..."
Emily Kingery

Table Of Contents

The Choice

Patricia Thrushart

The irony of choosing this over heaven—
this life of bone and blood; aches,
misses, mistakes; fleshy
covenants made and broken,
then made again; moments
of fleeting peace or petty
conflicts, of waning innocence
with wisdom hard-won;
the eternal optimism that
the Divine is waiting for you as if
you belong there and should never
have left in the first place,
but had no choice
as surely as dark briny oysters close
around a glowing, gritty pearl.

Memories Of Maps

Desiree Dufresne

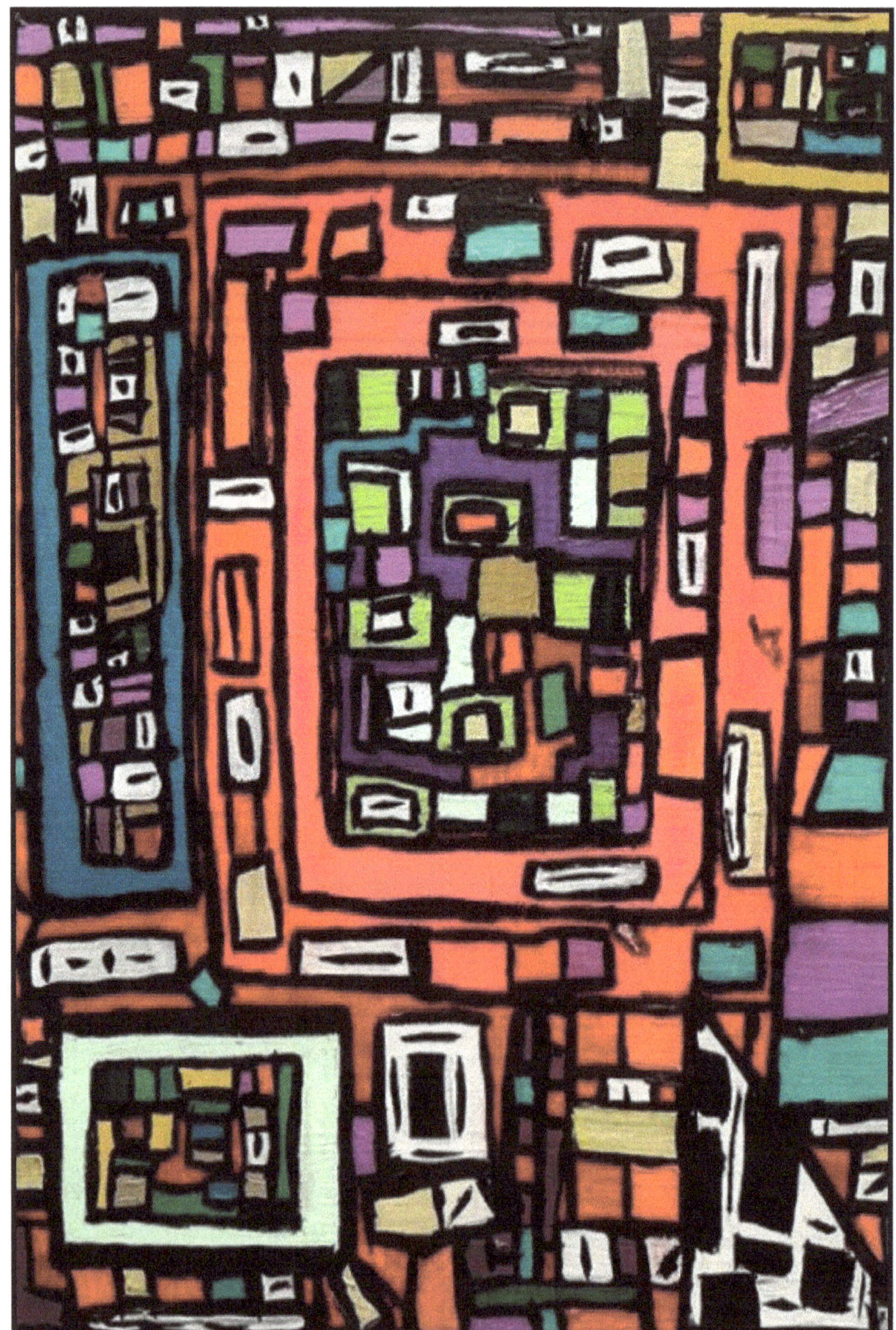

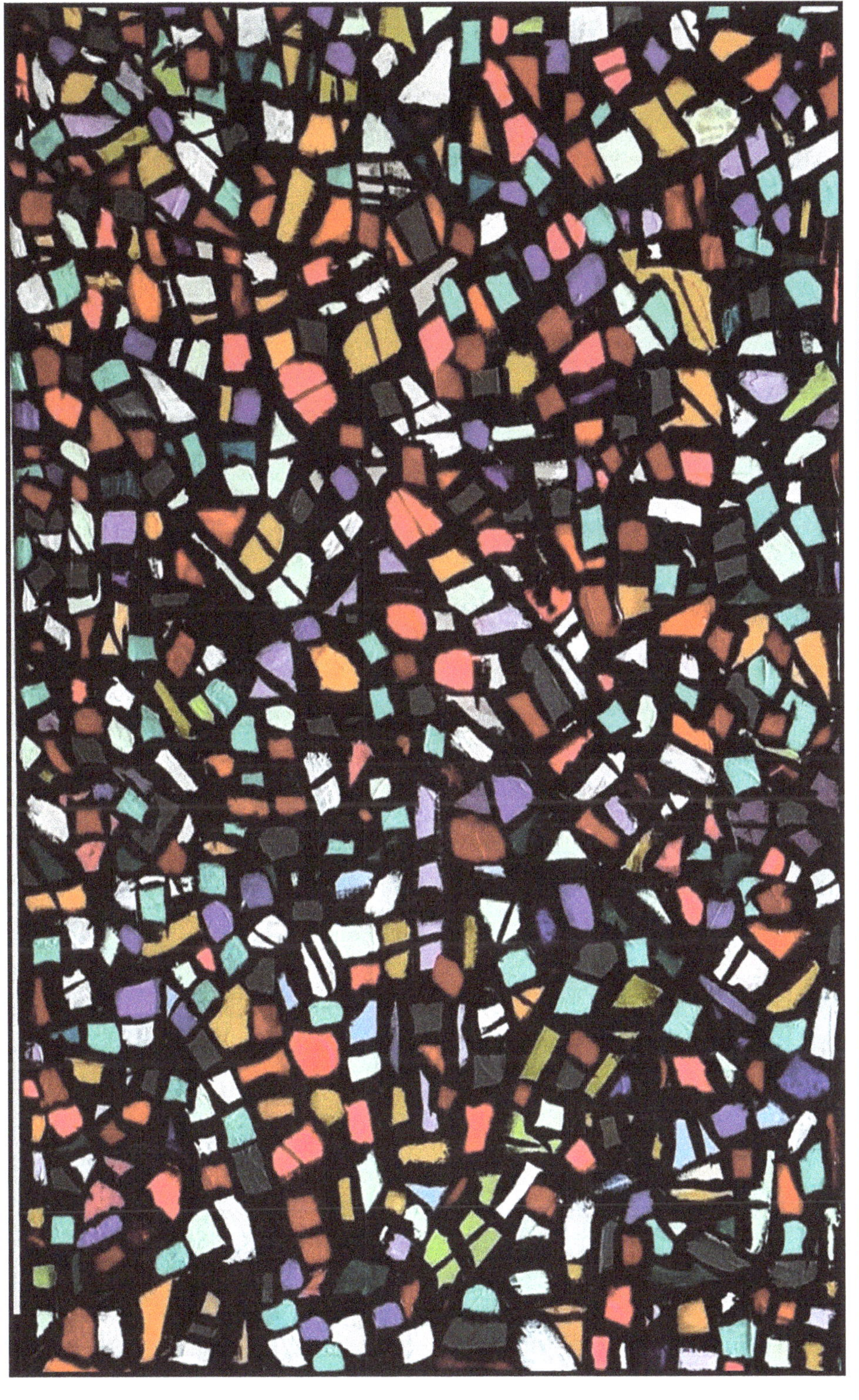

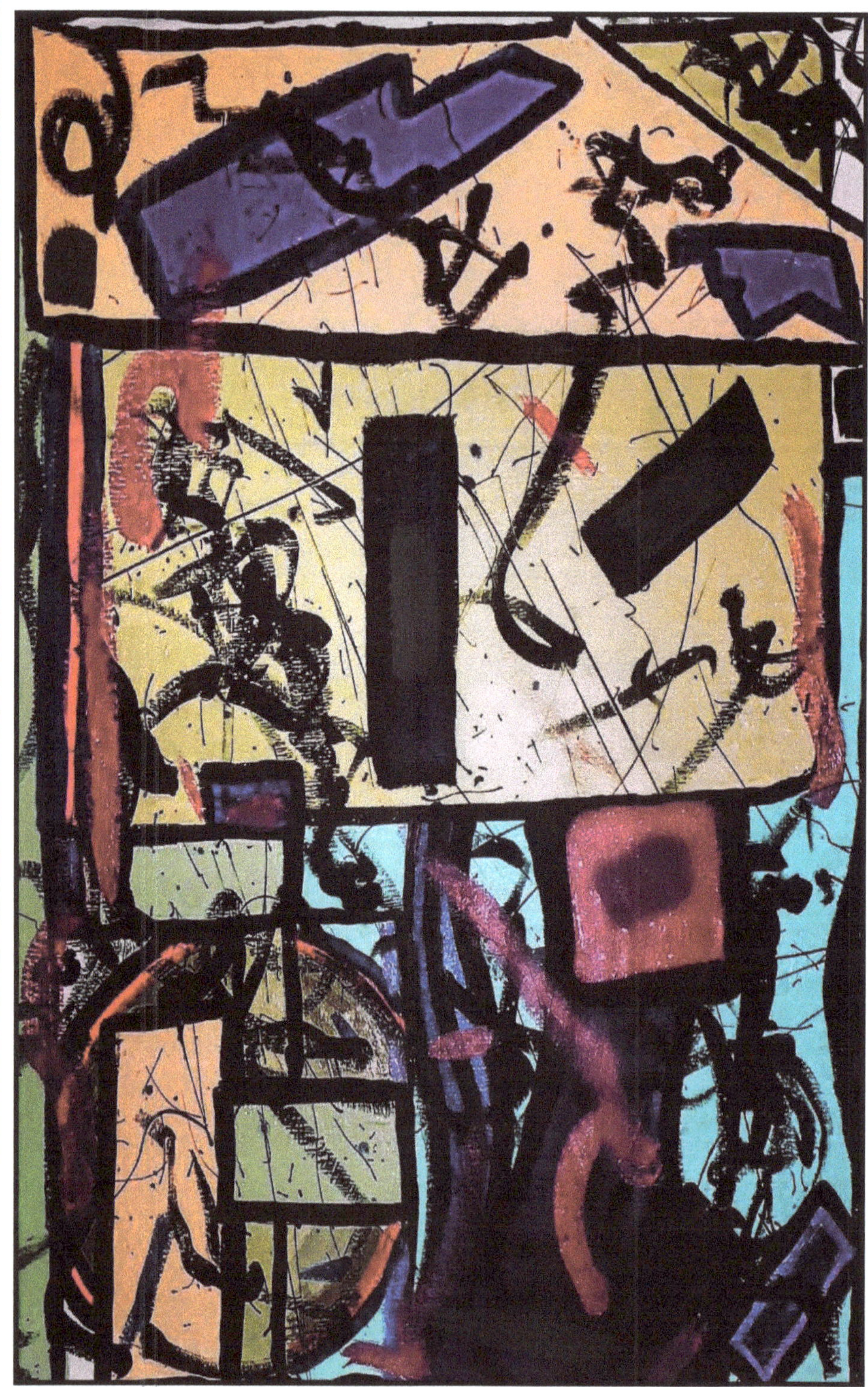

Lemme tell you bout that third eye

Kent Weigle

that one I been pickin at all this time

petals of breath
deliquesce in acetone
vertebrilliant viscereality
a shriven affectation
for my lioness

a memory frayed from too much use

I am the gray city that crumbles
where we been trepanning for gold
I read the intestines
of disenfranchised mice over breakfast

they tell us
démerdez-vous comme vous pouvez
it's your own damn
fault if you get
mugged by a nihilist

vagrance nonsense
system of collar bone smiles
system of katydid reflections
system of noseeums
eating up my ass

Alcoholism Is the Second Funniest Disease to Have

Nathaniel Hughes

your hair is always changing
to the background
of that nightly train rumble, whistle call.
passing by, screaming
loud,
falling in all the wrong places,
playing tricks
on yourself, leaving your clothes
in kitchen cabinets,
glasses behind window blinds,
making wrinkles in your face that will last forever.

Aeschylus, Bound (to Discourse):

Beatriz Seelaender

How Marxist Dialectics Helps Us Debunk The Myth Of Art When Thinking About Greek Tragedy, Something That Still Influences Us Ideologically Even Though We May Like Oedipus Be Blind To It

Aeschylus has always been a polemic figure. As the father of tragedy, he must be culpable for everything bad that has ever happened. As a playwright, he must be criticised due to the wrong message his theatre, more specifically *Oedipus*, may transmit about familial relationships. In this essay I will

crosswalk
Nikita Petrov

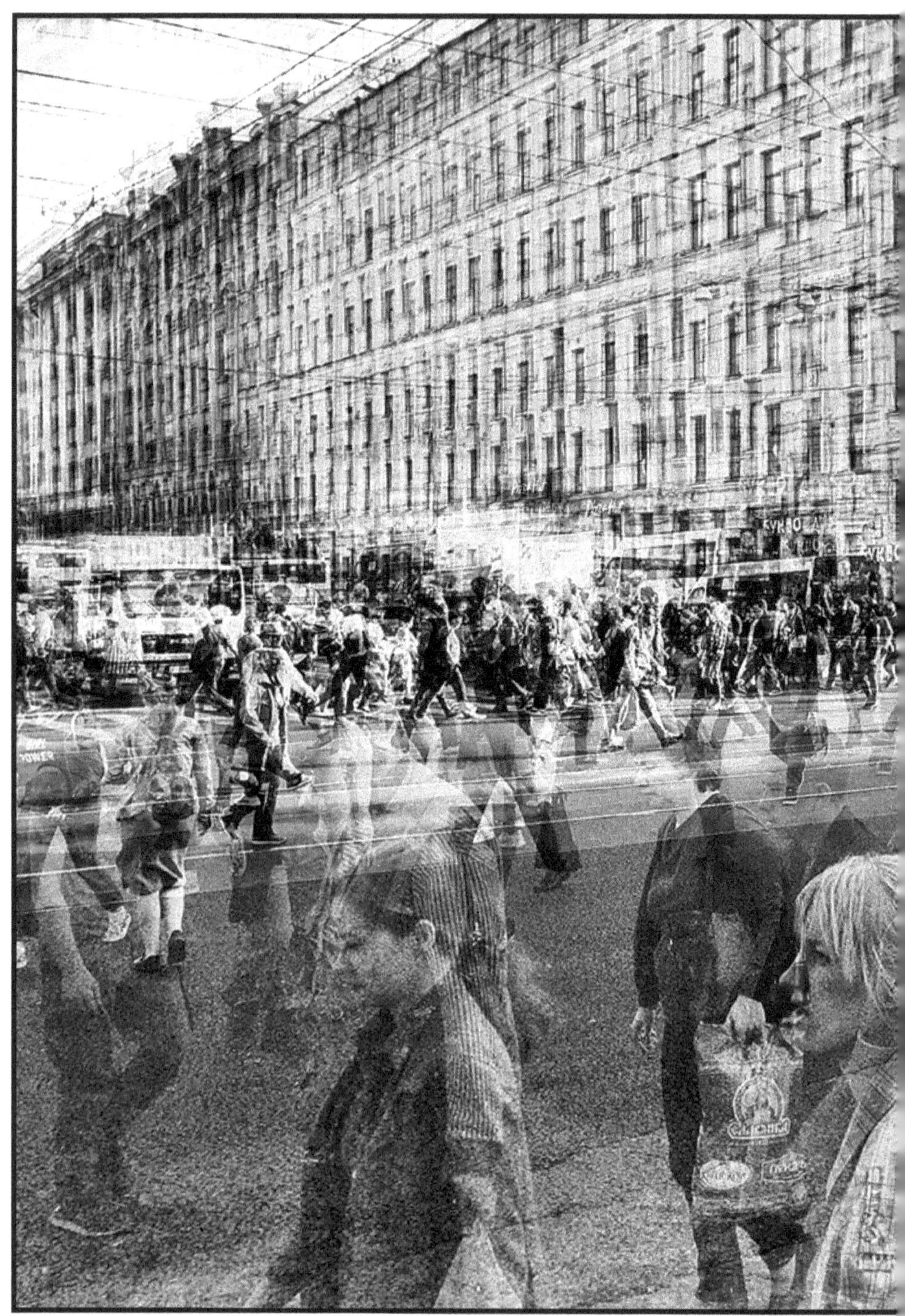

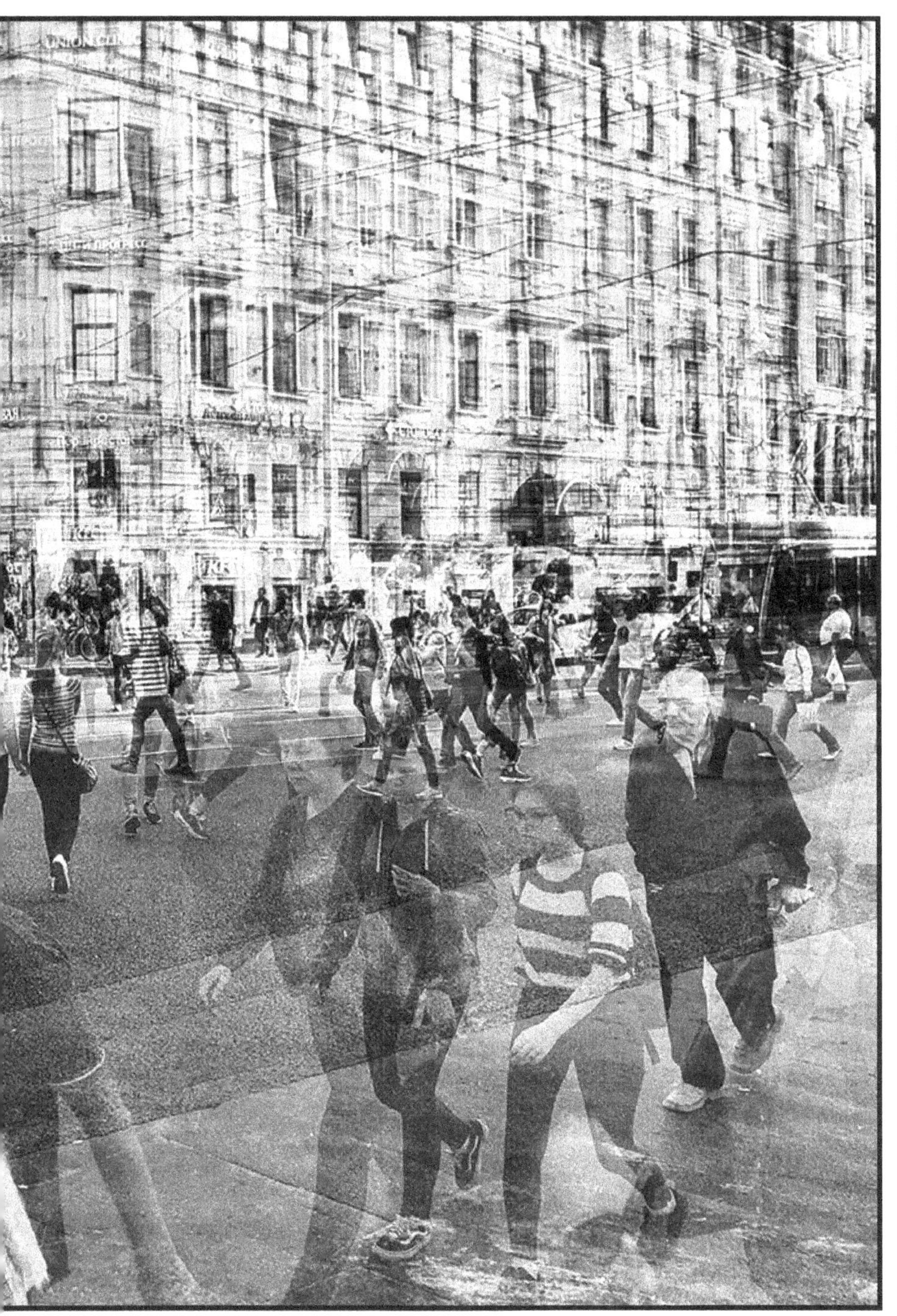

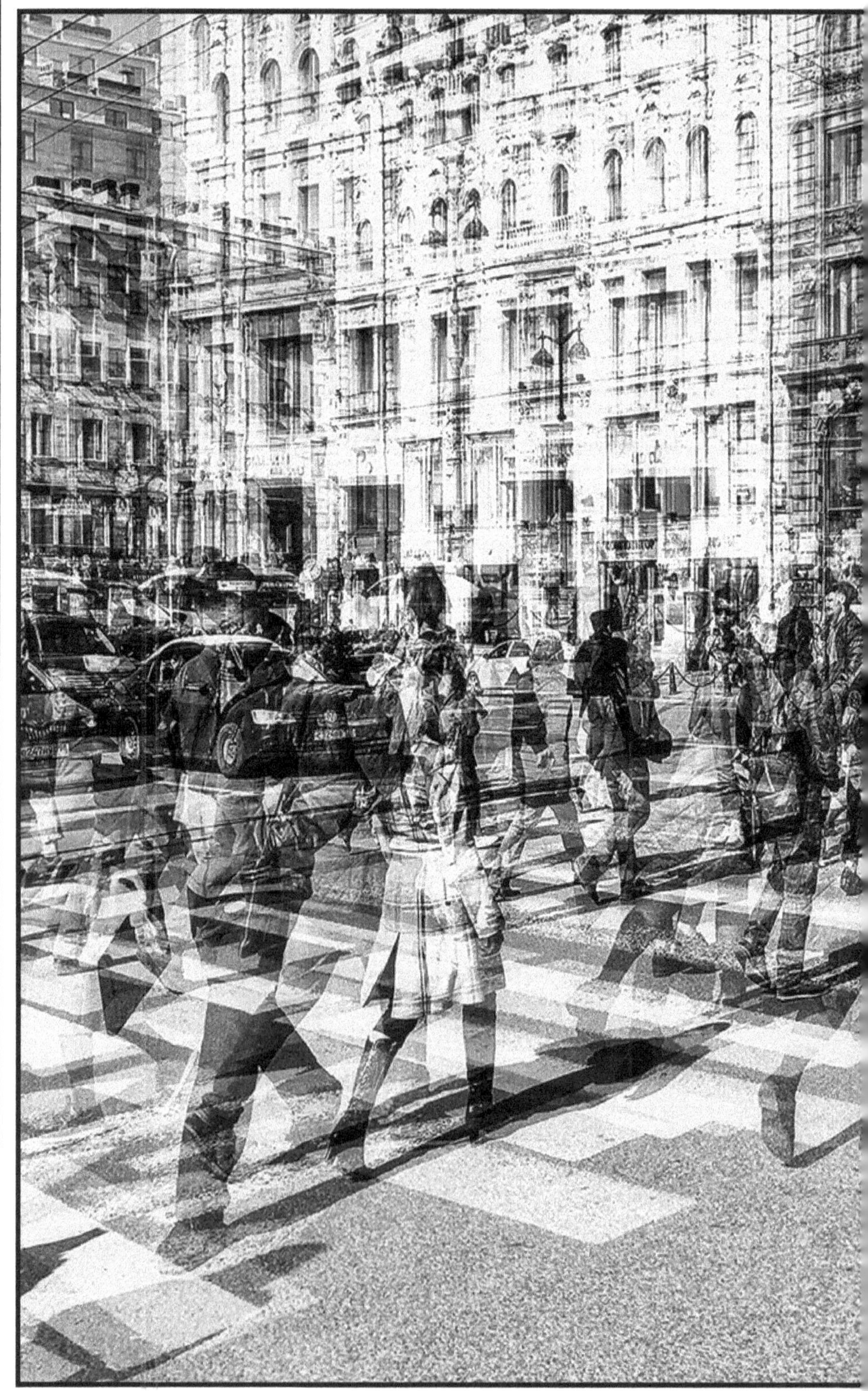

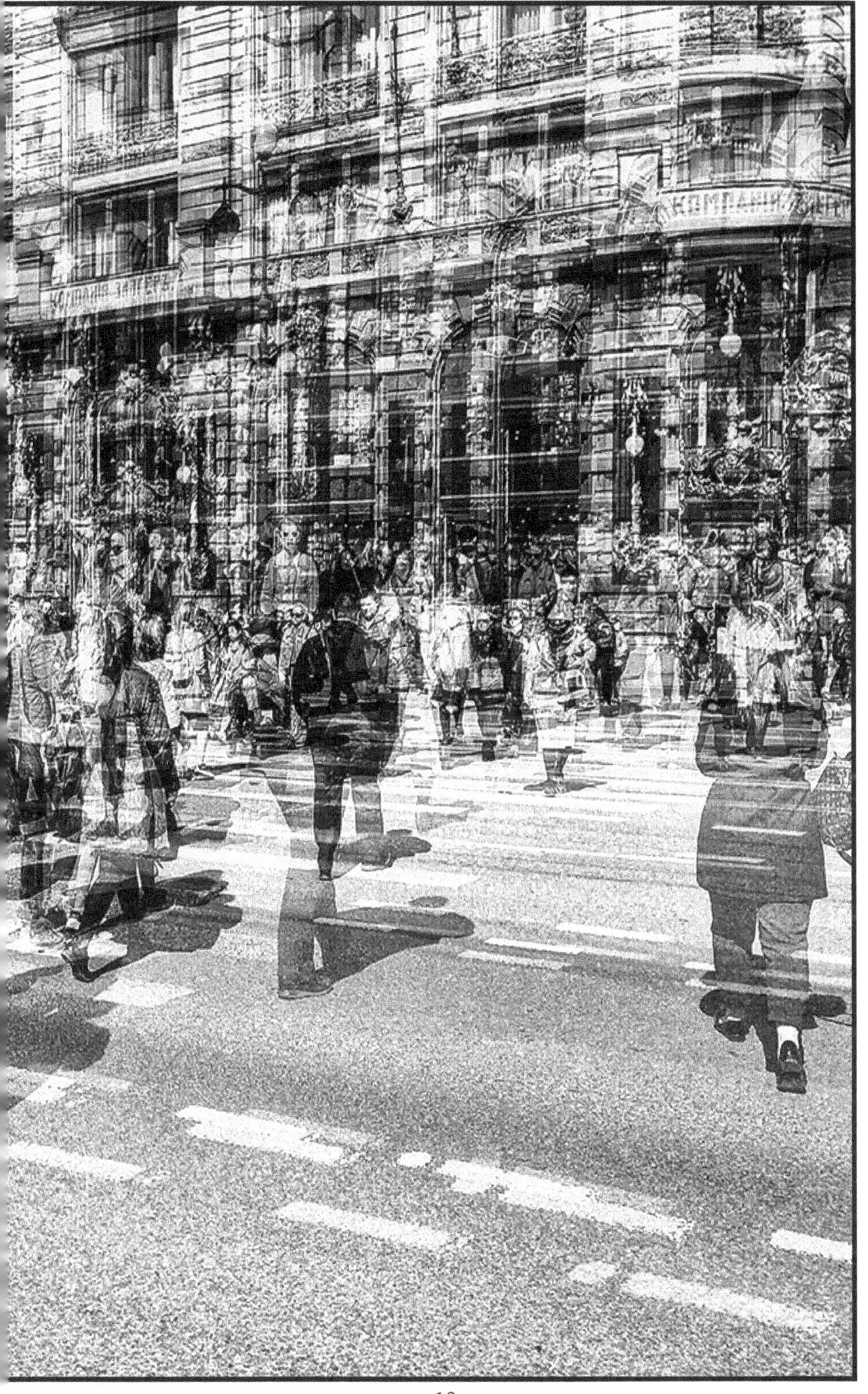

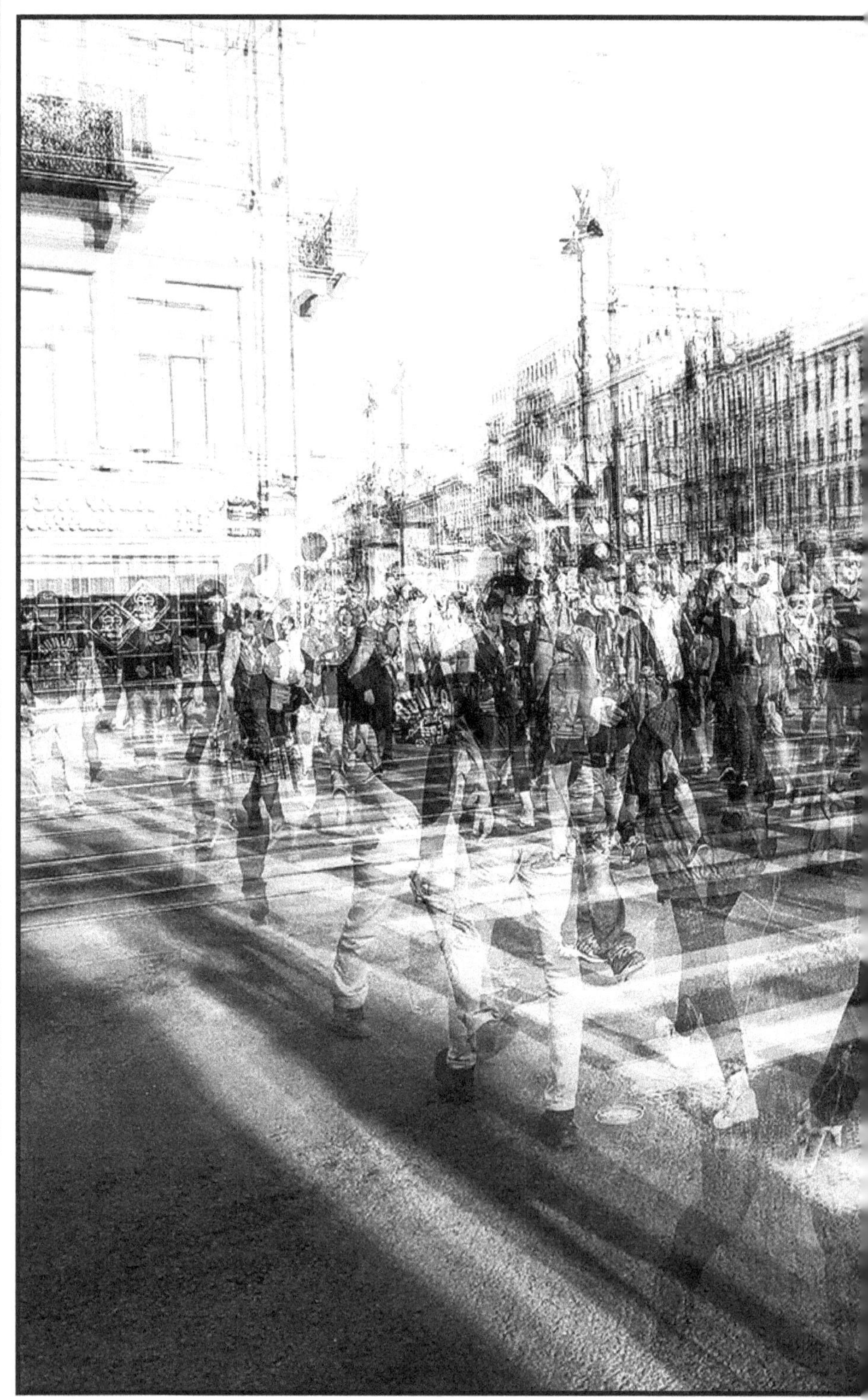

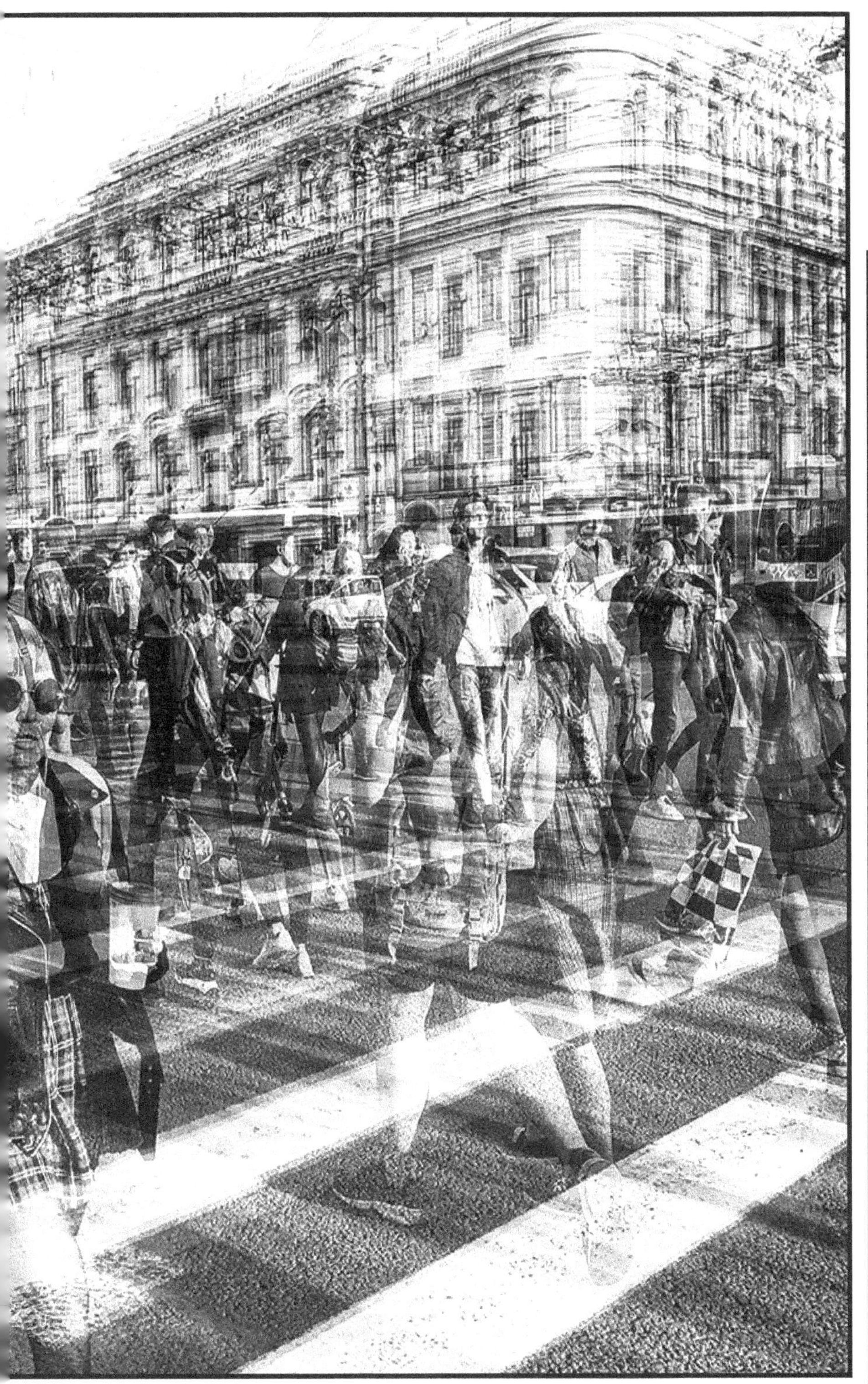

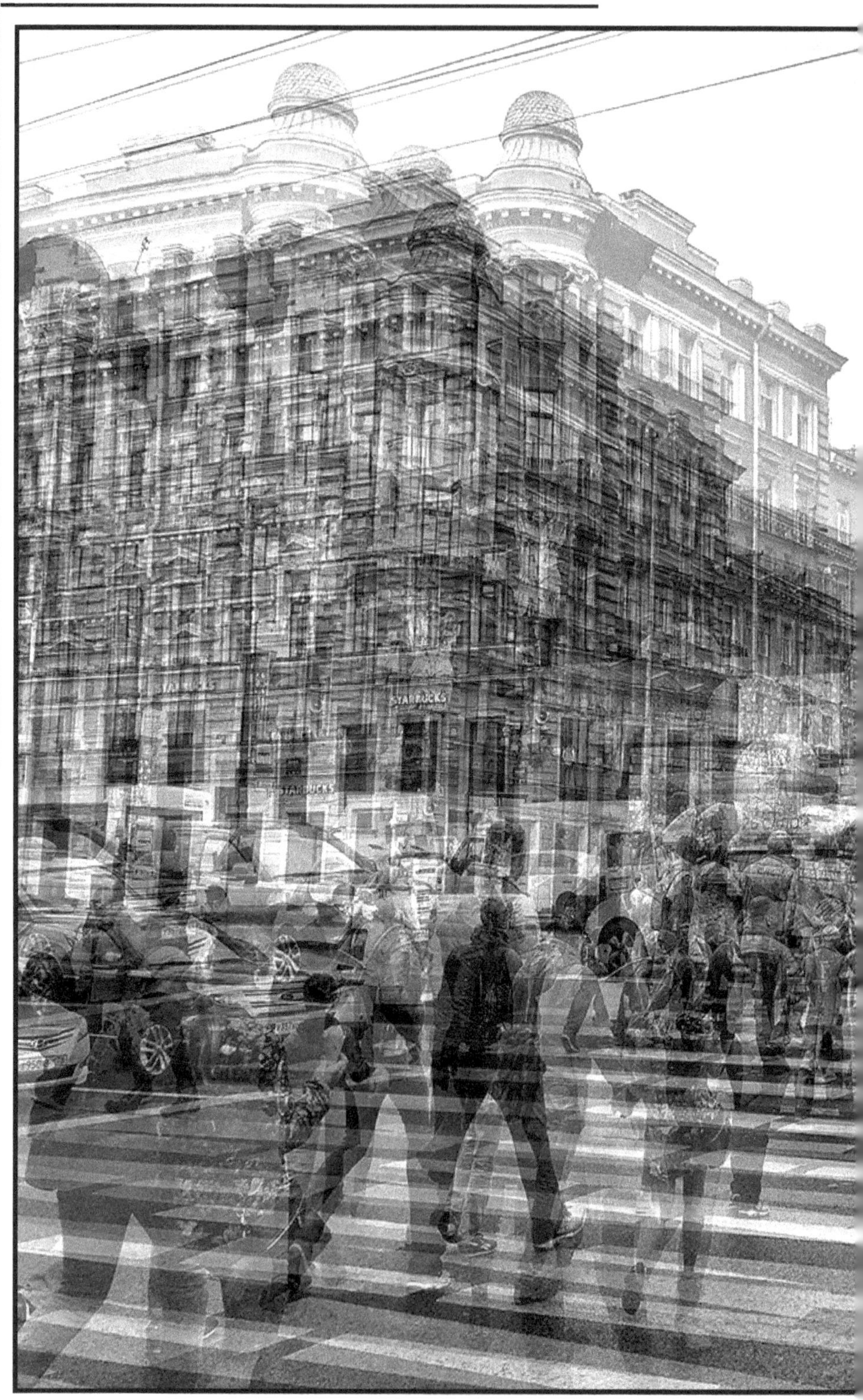

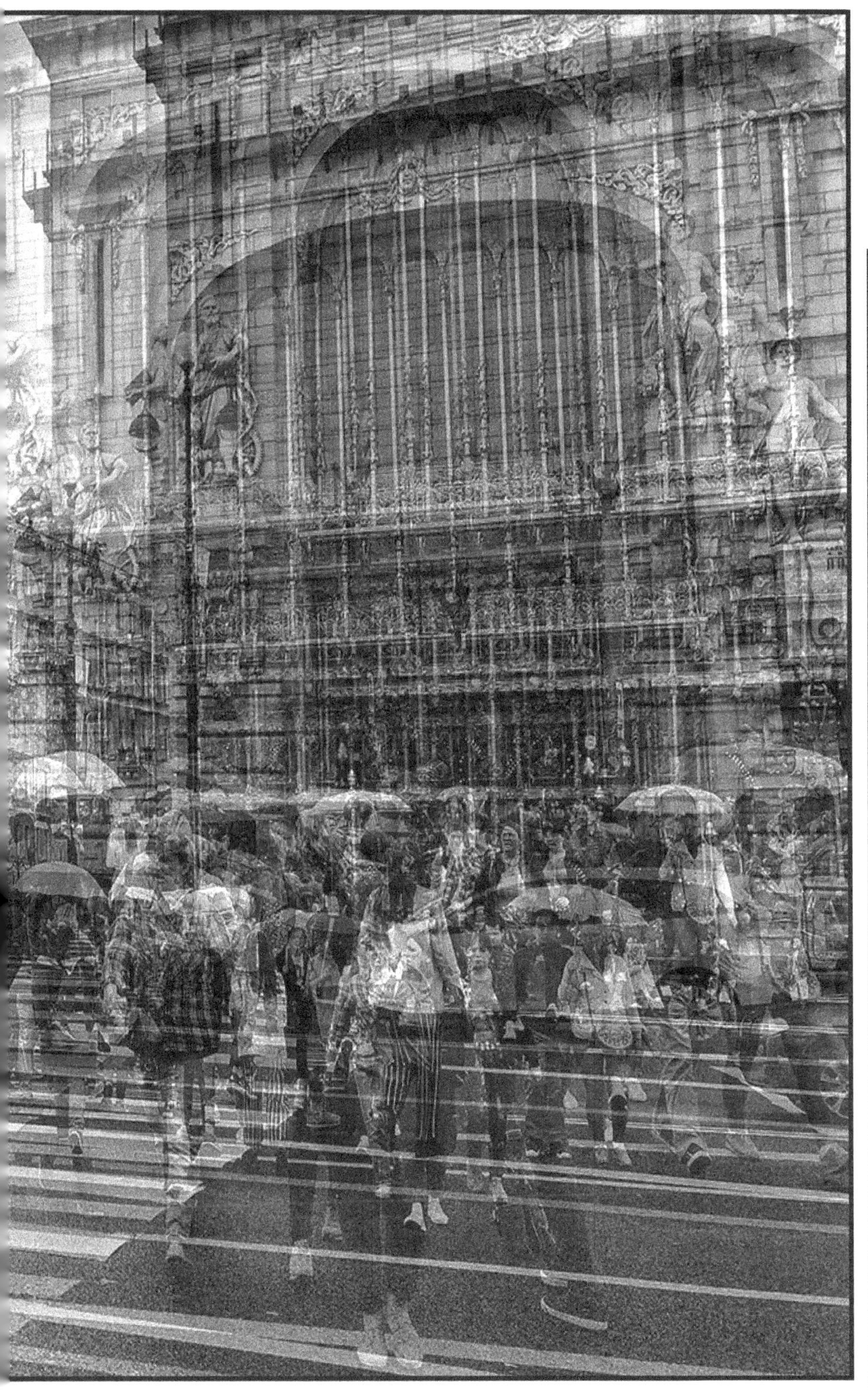

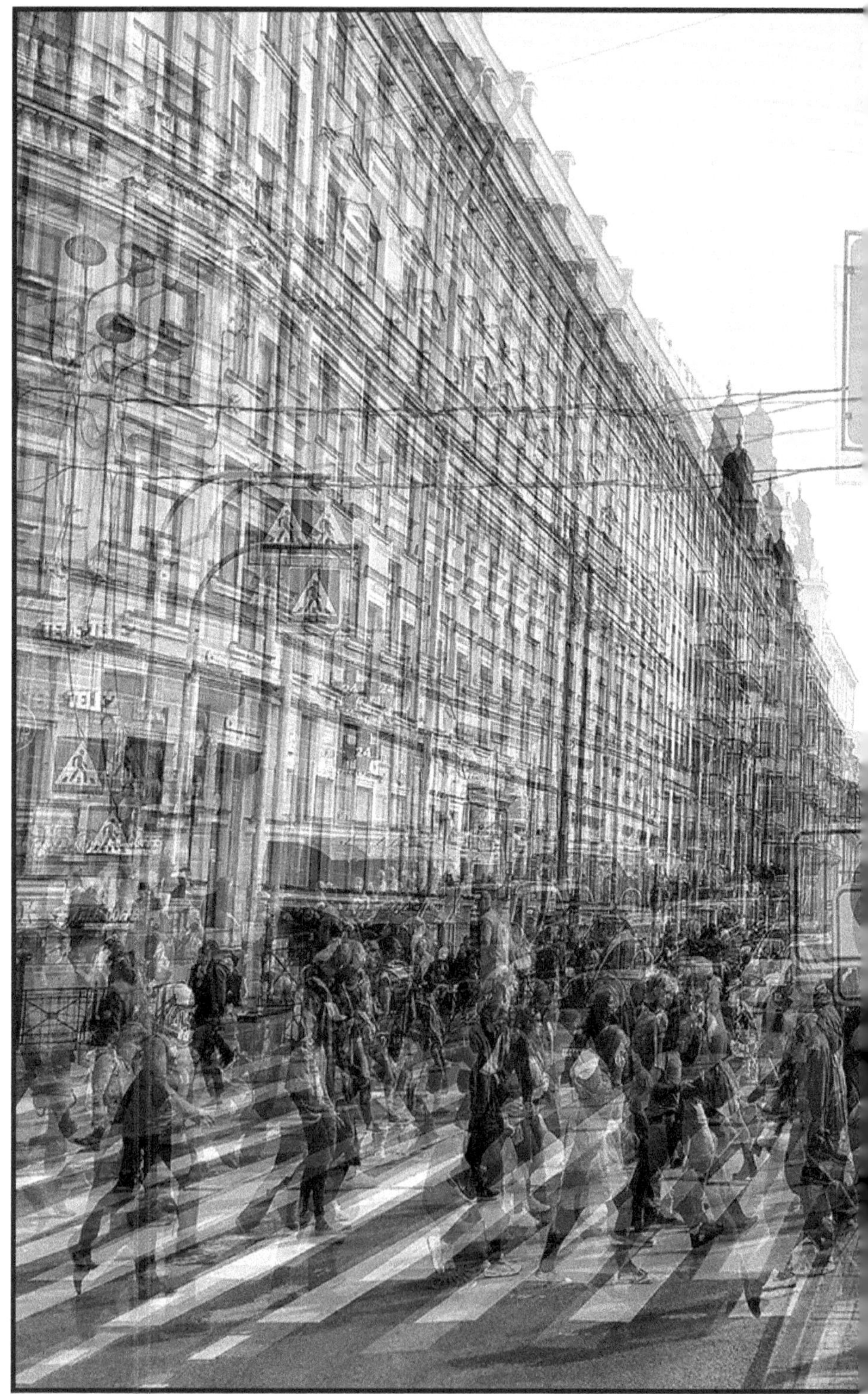

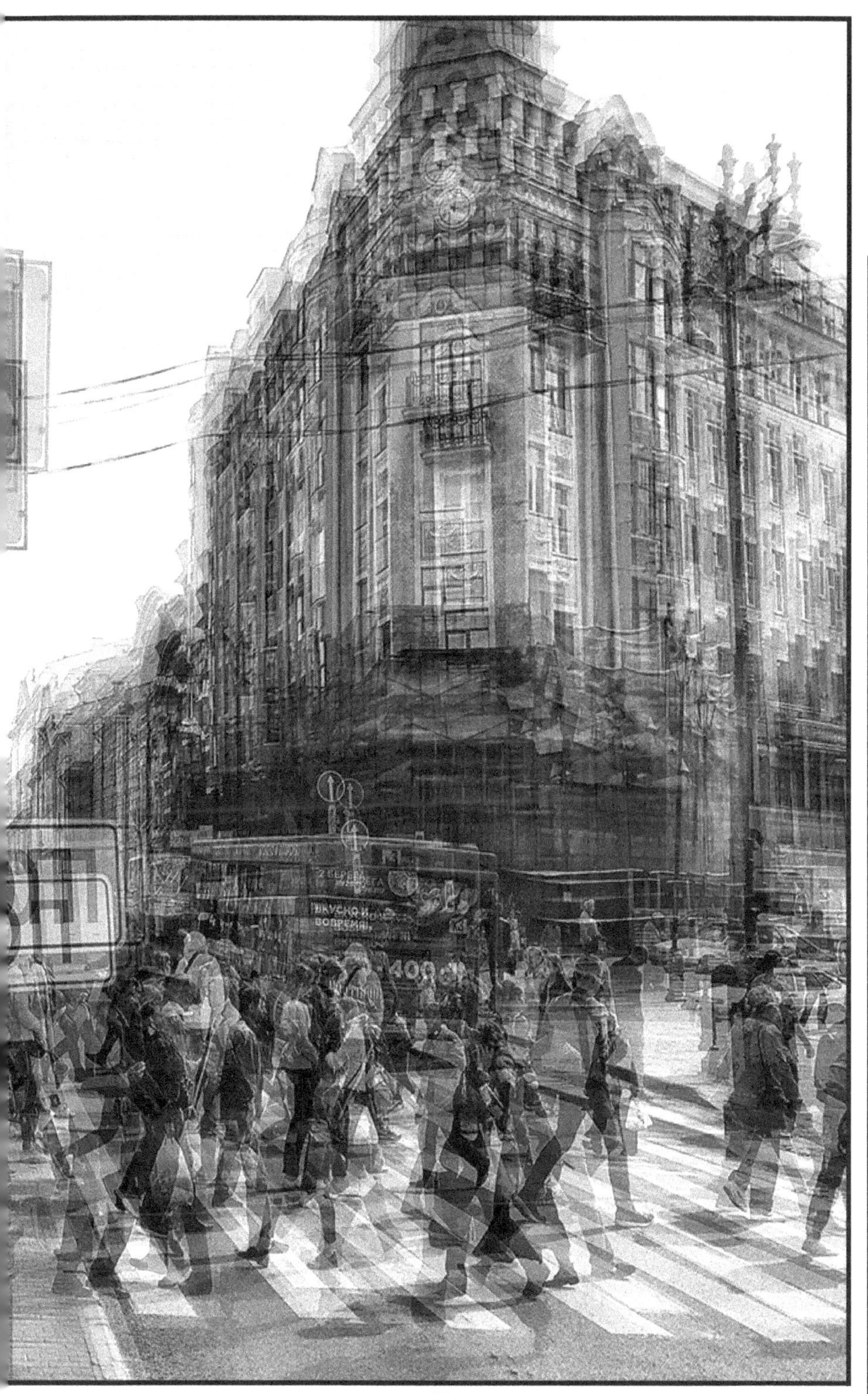

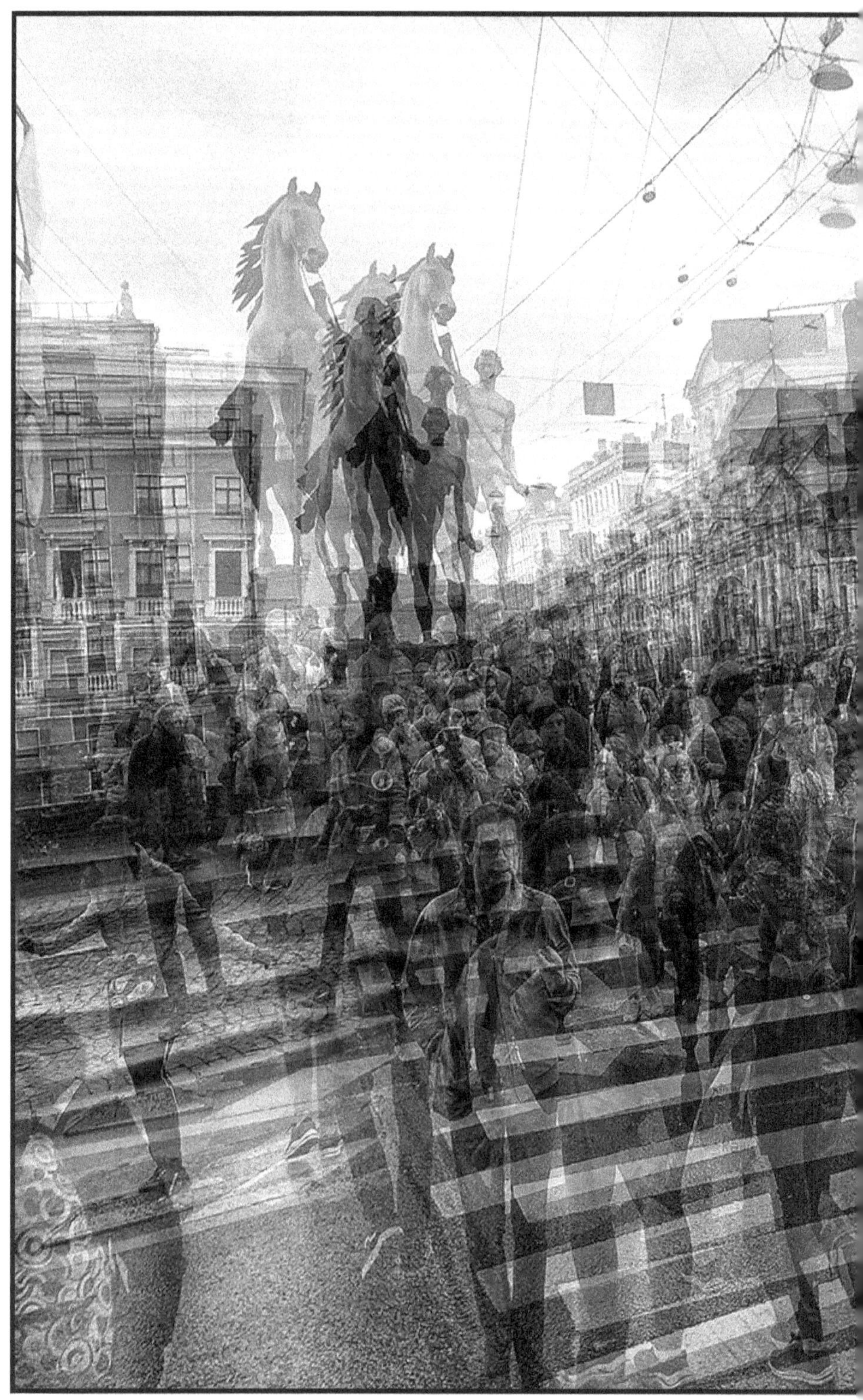

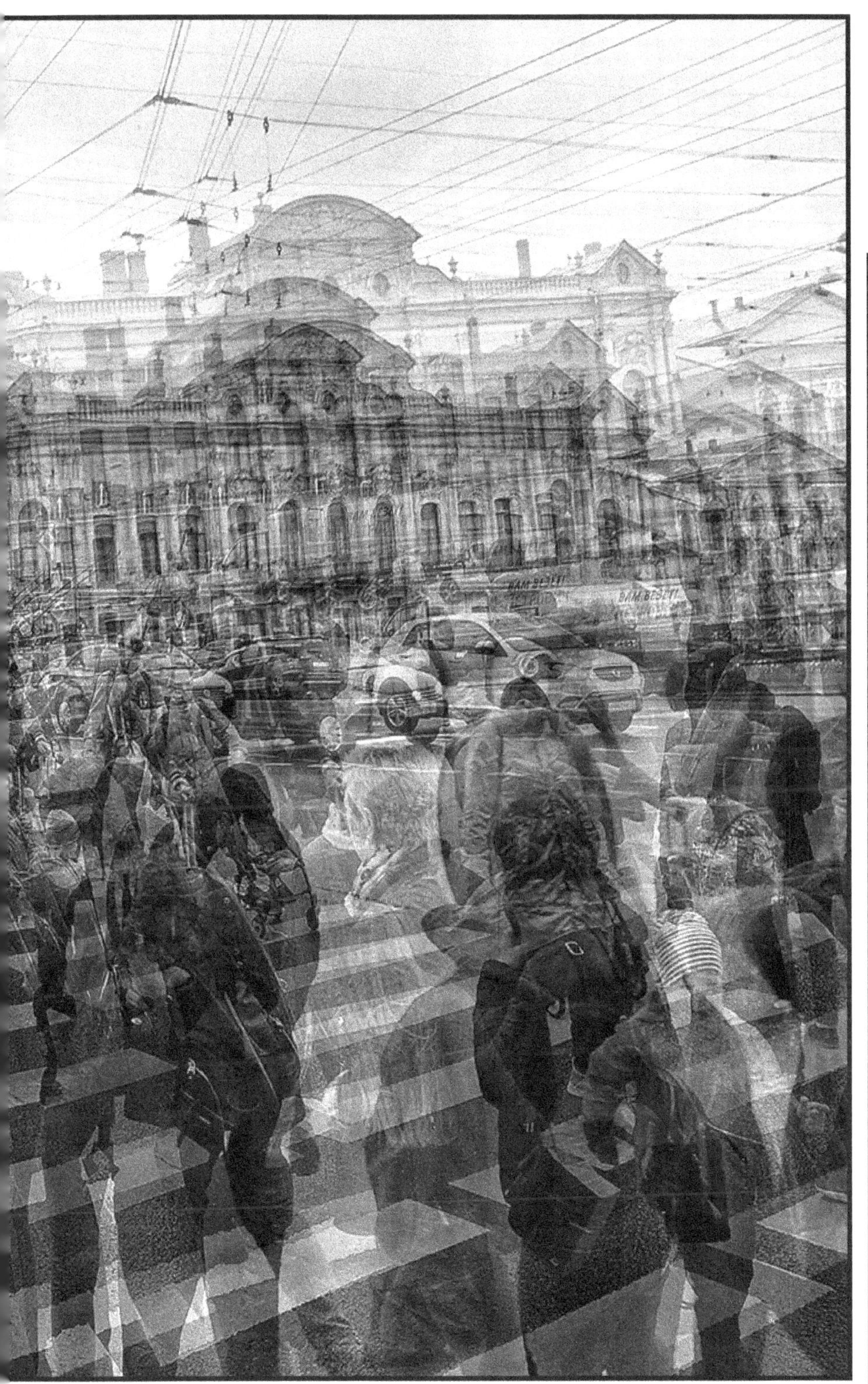

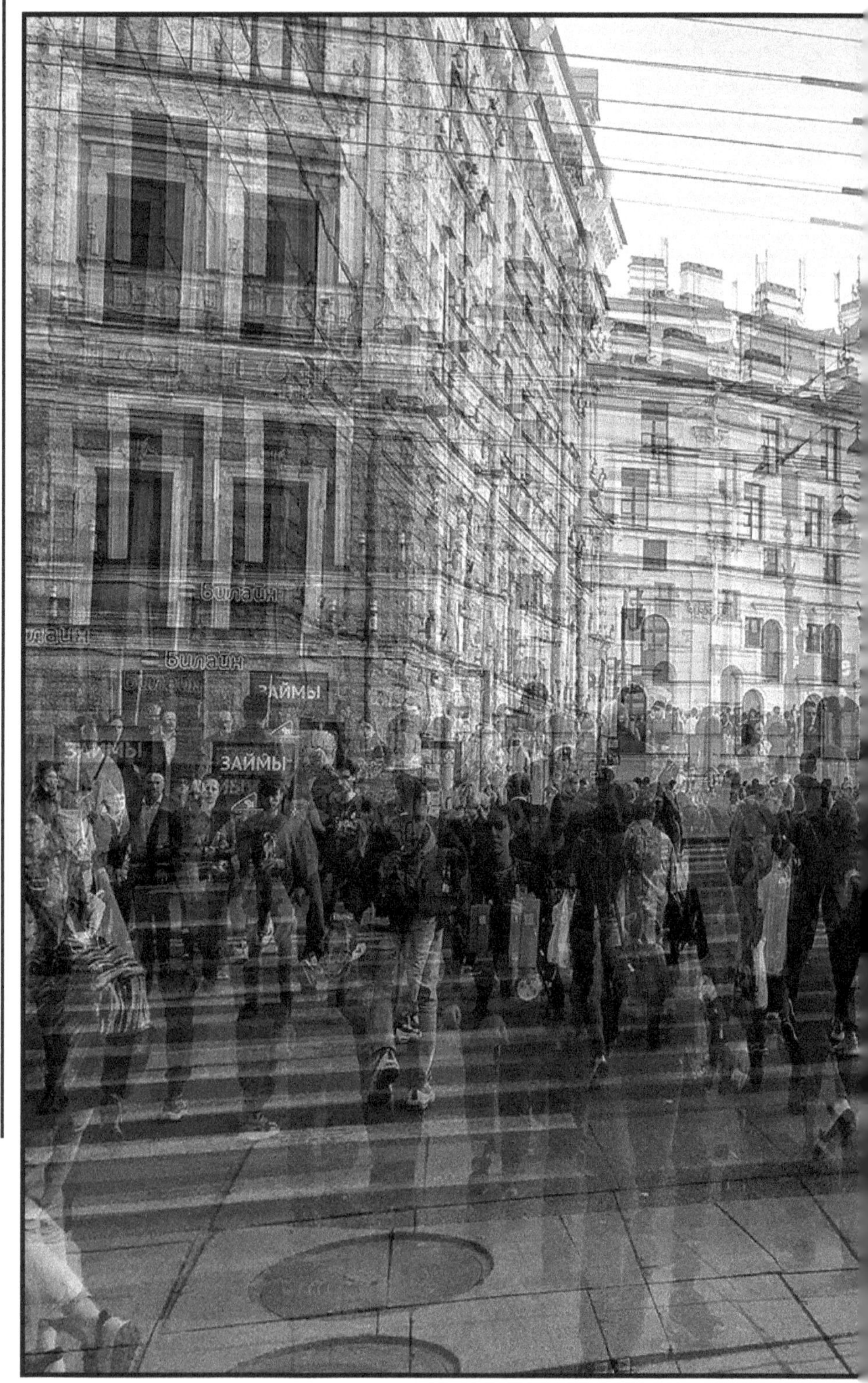

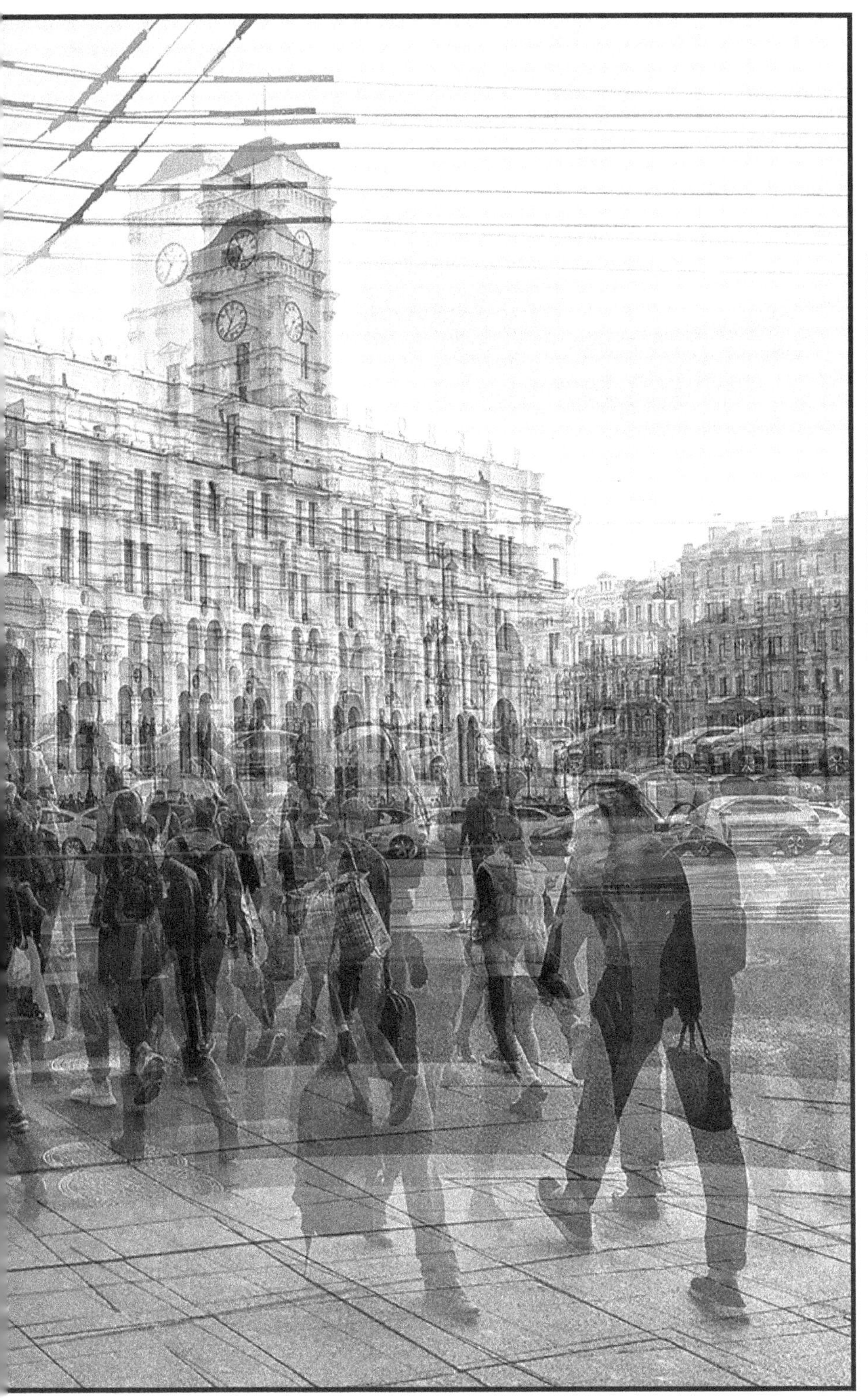

Exodus from halcyon

Felice Arenas

grief mocked acoustically.
I huddle I hope to ascend
beat back by photographs
of pine cellar doors, magma,
mothers swathing bisque dolls.
Where the hell where in Hell
do I knock around fire
to get a good look at Earth
as a particle? Remember Earth?
Wu Xing told of overcoming
or destruction—剋/克, *kè.*
Licking cobalt inside our cheeks
we waved we watched skies fold
sea floors like baby blankets.
Then a gasp a glance around.
Infernos have piped-in Muzak
believe it or not.

At the Library (for Grace Paley)

Mandy Clark

My son wants me to ask for the one about World War II
with a piano and a girl?
On the cover a kind of bird: white, he says.
After eleven years, I tell him to go ask himself
But the young woman, typing in a search for
another, lifts her finger to wait his turn.

A nickel short on the meter costs me a ten dollar ticket.
Today I found myself between the self-help and the children's section
At the edge of cartoon covers with teddy bears and
calico kittens whose parents drink too much.
There I was in the pictures, mother and daughter at once
Like paper dolls we wear each other's dresses.

And later, after a second bottle of cabernet sauvignon, I say
good job on finding the book you wanted.
He says, they didn't have that one. And your teeth are
red.

The Process of Becoming Homosexual

Michael Kreger

My likeness transitions
across my self
past boundaries within my ego
my interior sex is in confusion
as if midnight movie elbows touching
fucking across a plastic divide
stoned from a blowjob and weed
exhaling a millennium
of oppression and inquisition
and disapprovingly tight lips
with the desire for death (and life)
misaligned remembrances
hot and cold
and salted tongues
under skin and blood
pounding my chest into haze
spreading myself
across the globe
exposing guts and glory
shame and warm skin
writing myself into something
curved like a signature's end
cut right down the middle;
two perfect halves
a whisper between lips and teeth
within a single breath
a multitude of sonnets
and silicone breasts
on fire as I flame
illuminate me in Jesus
bring me back from the dead in a gay bar
three days later.

flamingo dances

Laura Mota

at night I have to remind the body
it is still mine.

as if I'd never left
it waltzes alone as it used to do
in our flamingo dances.

disobedient to new music,
it moves out of sync with new partners.

because the twirls of Laguna Brava
cannot be undone
my mouth whispers to me
in a motherly presage tone.

the twirls of Laguna Brava
cannot be undone.

my body searches for his height
his hands, his chest to lay after the dance.
it is impetulant to time and place,
it ignores my despair.

the twirls of Laguna Brava
cannot b...

I press my lips to avoid the spell.
I hinder my body with a bottle of wine.
at night I have to remind it
you're still mine.

Sundress

Paris Weslyn

With broad brushstrokes the unfolding of the world is painted in the blinking eyes of dawn.

The heavens are shrouded by layers upon layers of gray, wool-like and vaporous, with flickers of silver which loom across the horizon, and are held up by the outstretched arms of towering fir and pine.

The Sun remains cloaked and hooded behind them all. She is coy and shows off neither ankle, wrist, nor elbow. Her radiance is hidden under the paleness of day. The heads of mountains are covered by the foggy hem of her skirts, and at their feet water—cold and clear— ripples across the bones of the Earth, filling up his veins.

Breach

ky li

Salty waves break atop my freckled feet.
Sand gives way under my sinking heels.
Any residual bare skin is winnowed
in grey fog before a protesting sea.

Age has crumbled into tides that wear
down stone & shell, & bone quelled into
unrecognizable particles that still dance.

Women & men dissolve into a breach
that opens & closes like a batting eye.

Watered down fractions of time
ripple away into swallowing current
& are thrashed onto shore,
whose only desire in life is to lie
peacefully amid other battered souls.

The Looking Glass

Ami J. Sanghvi

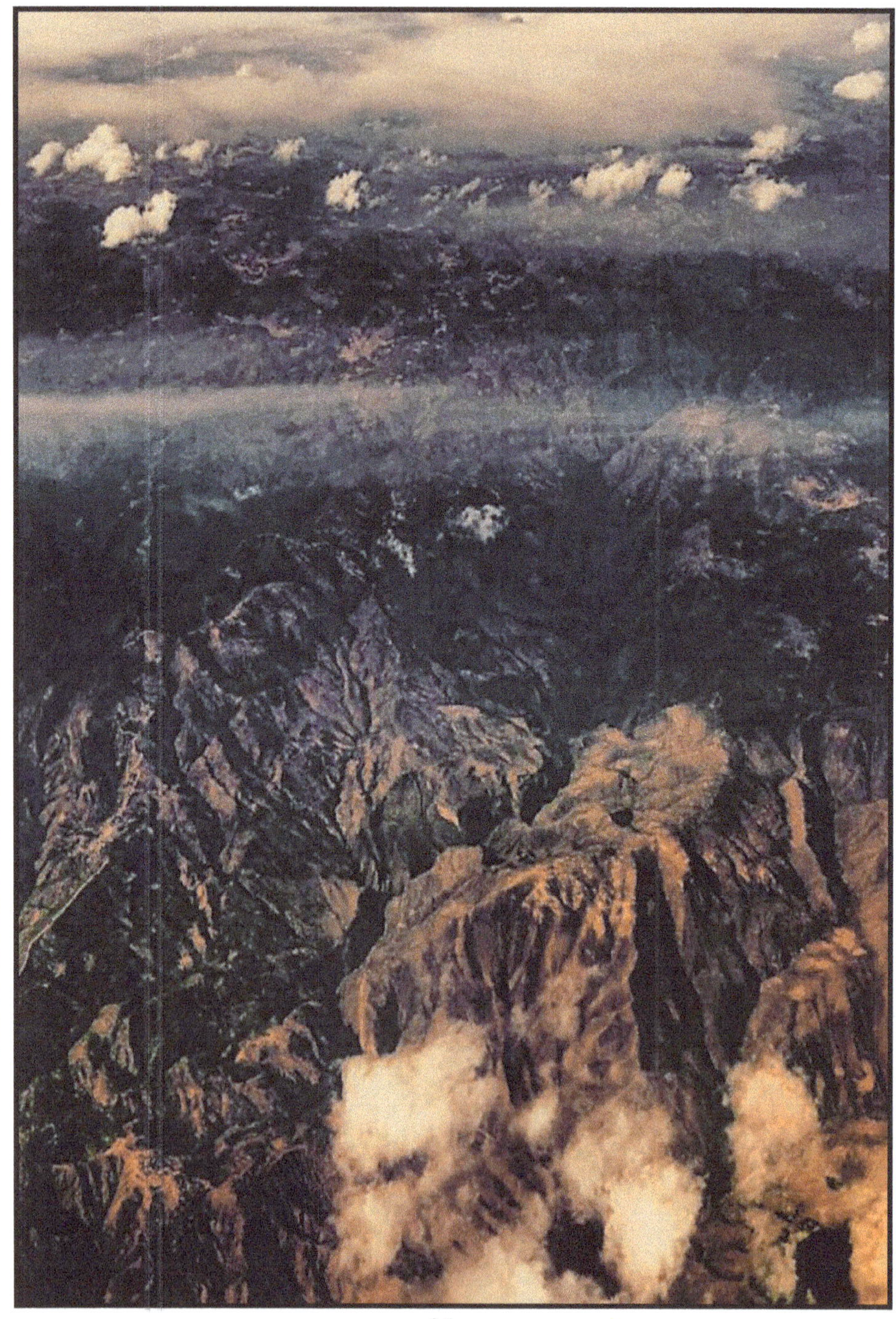

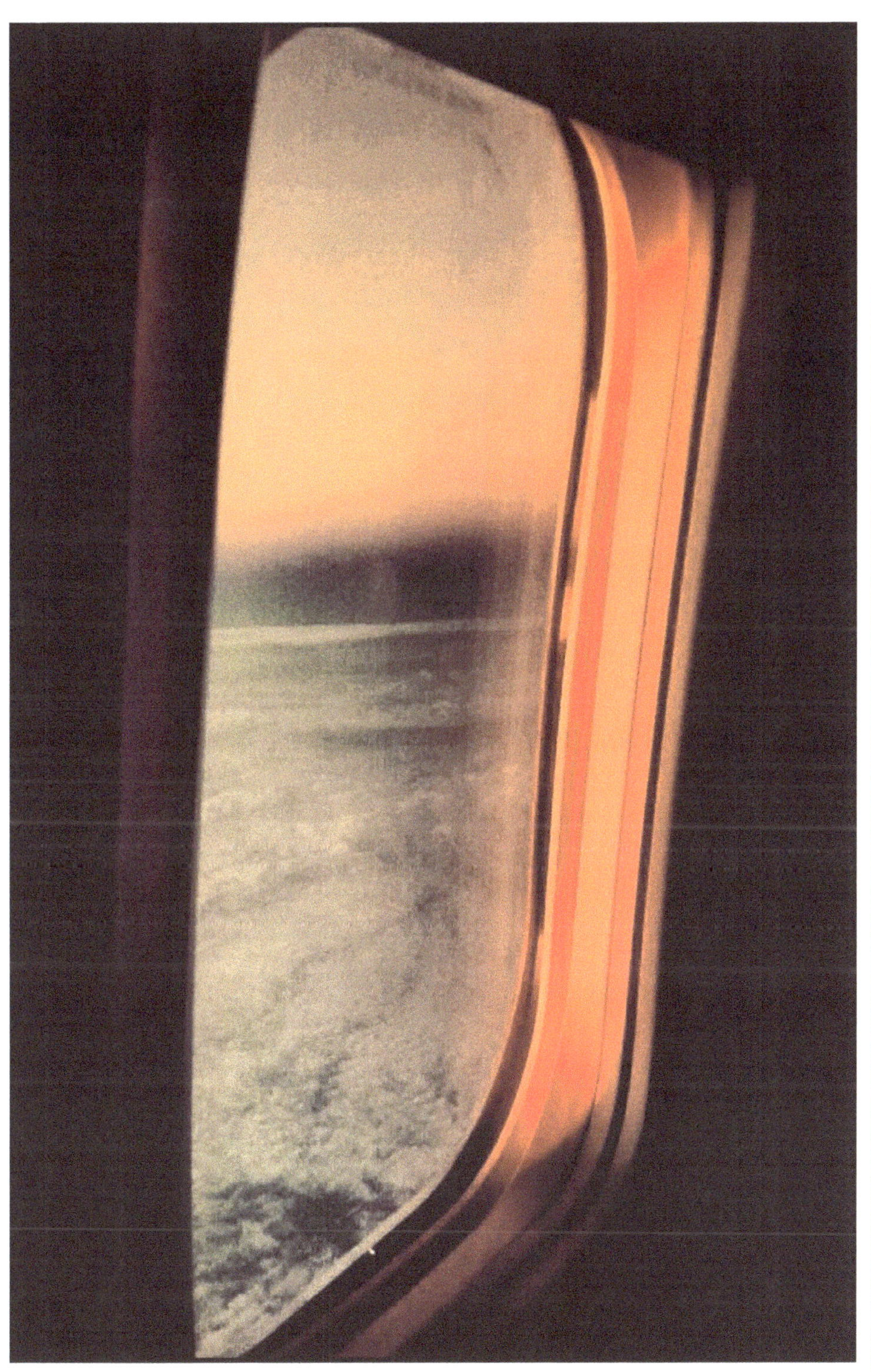

Darwin's Islands of the Arabian Sea

M. SHAYNE BELL

Second
Galapagos,
but more mysterious—
how to classify the phoenix:
burning,

dying—
but then reborn;
or classify the djinn:
a man or a woman—but then
incense

falling
into bottles,
scent like apple blossoms
pervading the space. Yes, Darwin
hinted

magic.
Einstein's paper
on the subject called them
cosmological unconstants.
Dark force,

magic—
they are wonders!
I will not ignore them,
for the phoenix does burn and live
again;

the djinn
do transform, then
make three wishes come true.
I would ask for ever-blooming
tulips,

then wait
ten years to ask
a second wish: then wait
twenty years thinking hard about
the third.

Could I
bring back the dead?
With one wish or with three—
forget tulips—whom would I choose
to bring?

Her

Patrick Wang

In 9th grade I stared into a
mirror and waged a war with
the boy I saw shattered along
edges of American manhood
sealed off by narrow walls
of conquest and violence
as I reached its pearly gates
other men entered carrying
their dictionaries of cruelty
"damn you fucking killed *her*"
"let's fuck the shit out of *her*"
her has no place in this society
her is a mere game of
smash or pass
"Pass *her*? I'd smash *her*"
in this society men communicate
through clenched teeth
"no homo"
to excuse touch but all I see
are little boys learning to say
"not human"
"I am not human"
"You are not human"
"*her* is not human"
her is a crippled doe
lying lifeless across
man's shoulder
the prize of war

That once broken boy I saw
never entered those
barbed wire gates
the price was too great
I refused to give up
my humanity
he/him/his
masculinity is mine to
define:
"I am human"
"You are human"
"She is human."

THE PLANTS EYE

Valyntina Grenier

This is speculation I know but
idol flowers have always born
our mean making scissors
Consider scissors nature's troop
deploying astonishing devices

The pitcher
marooned and white
not attractive unless
you reinforce the species
in question *mimicry*
intended to scare
the Victorians
the arc of corseted breasts
crowned w/ clitoria

Consider an insect
evolved to conceive
as female and male tantalizingly
from behind

Call the behavior
pseudo-copulation
call the flower
prostitute
A frenzy of intercourse
ensures pollination

Our factory
is olfactory tactile attention
to not just simple chemicals
signals so far as creatures are things
to secure pollination or a meal
It's in our sanctum

As we rush around mounting
disseminating genes
flowers traffic metaphor
a meadow brims
with our making

Move the garden
Multiply
Flowers take aim
Secure/ obscure notions long ago
crossed our own offspring

That match the
symbiosis of desire
fire in the garden

Quixotic

Jerome Berglund

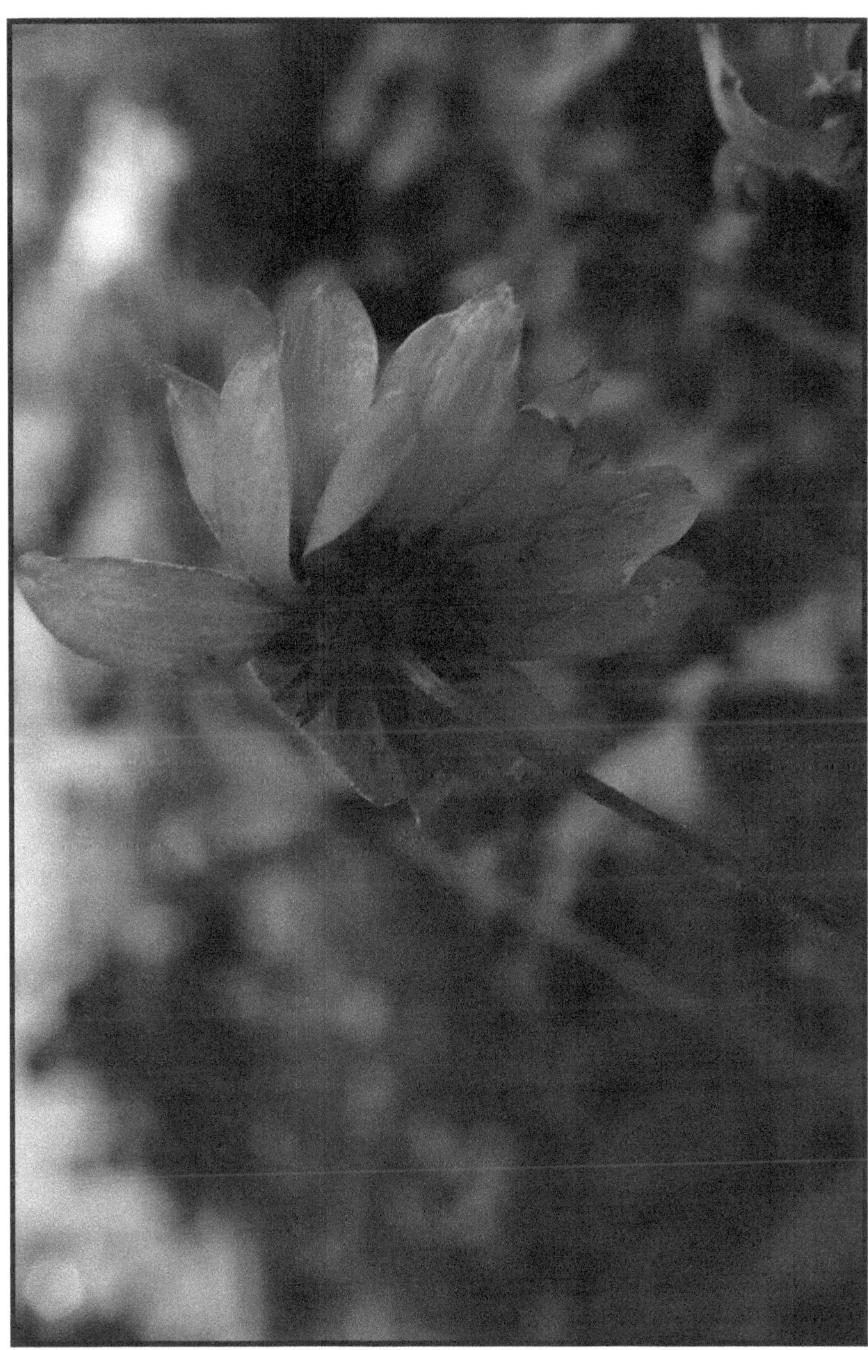

La Mancha

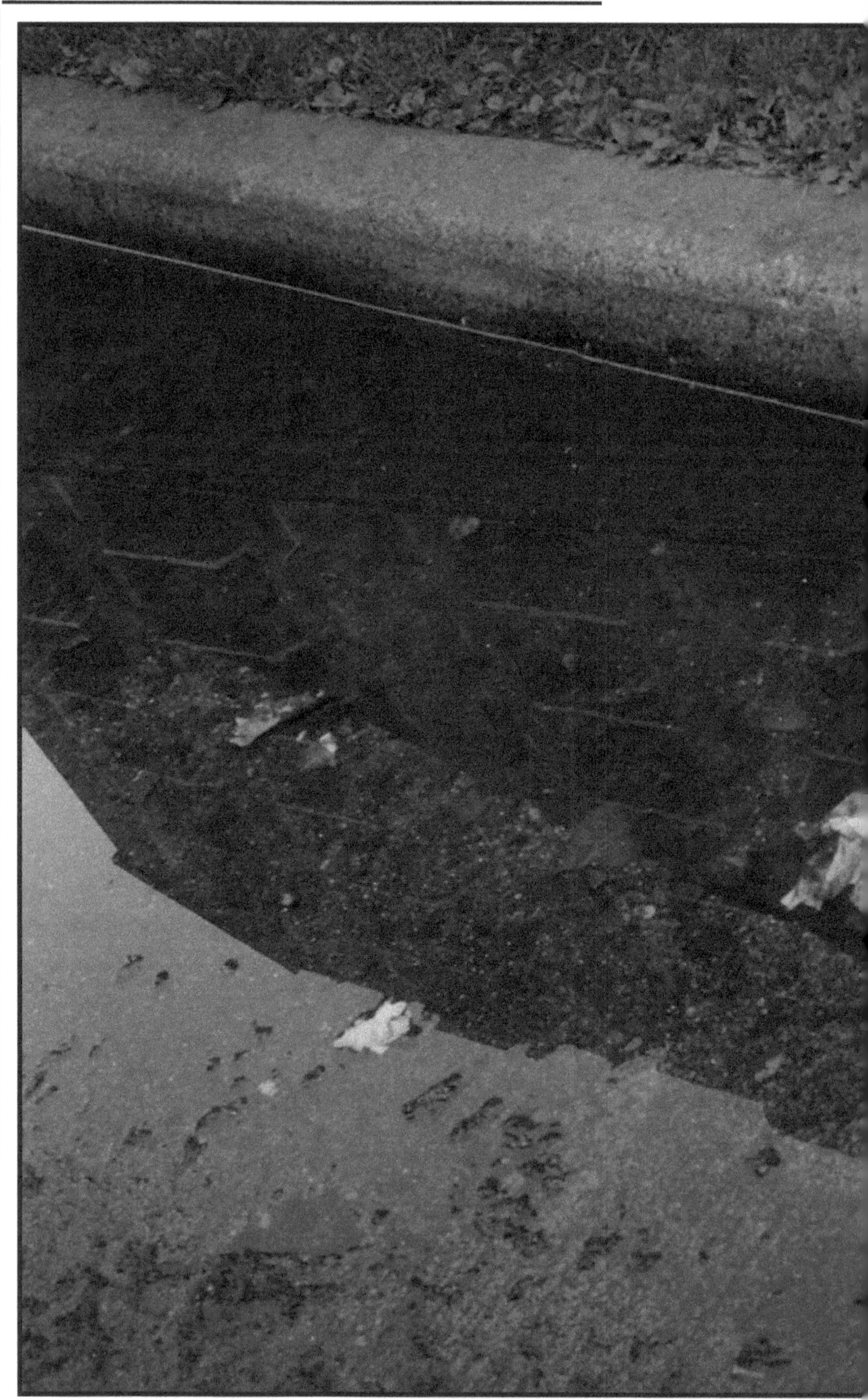

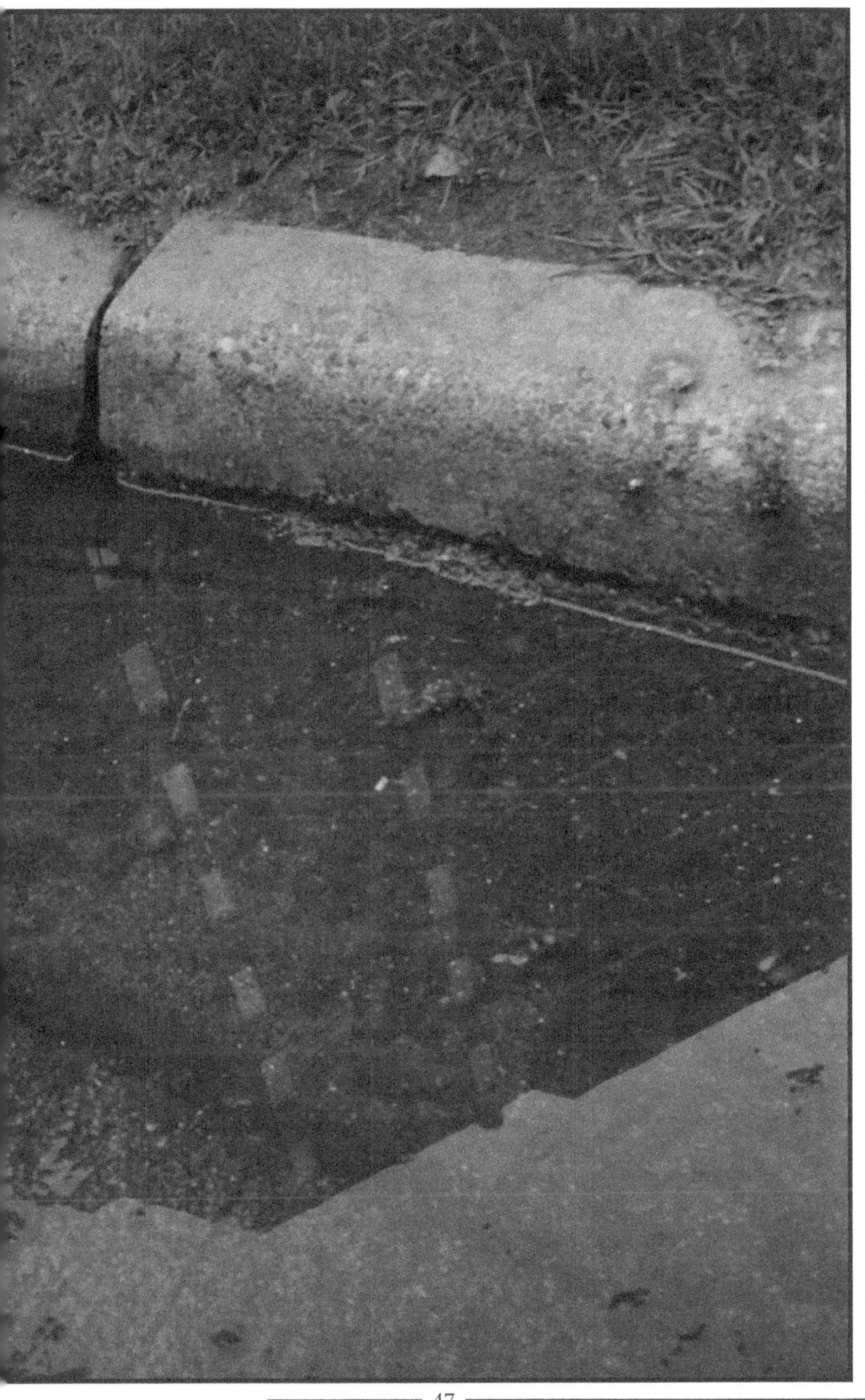

touch

Sasha Torchinsky

my father never touched me
or held me as a baby
his childhood dictated his fatherhood
when he dies i will touch him
for the first time

untitled
yeting xiong

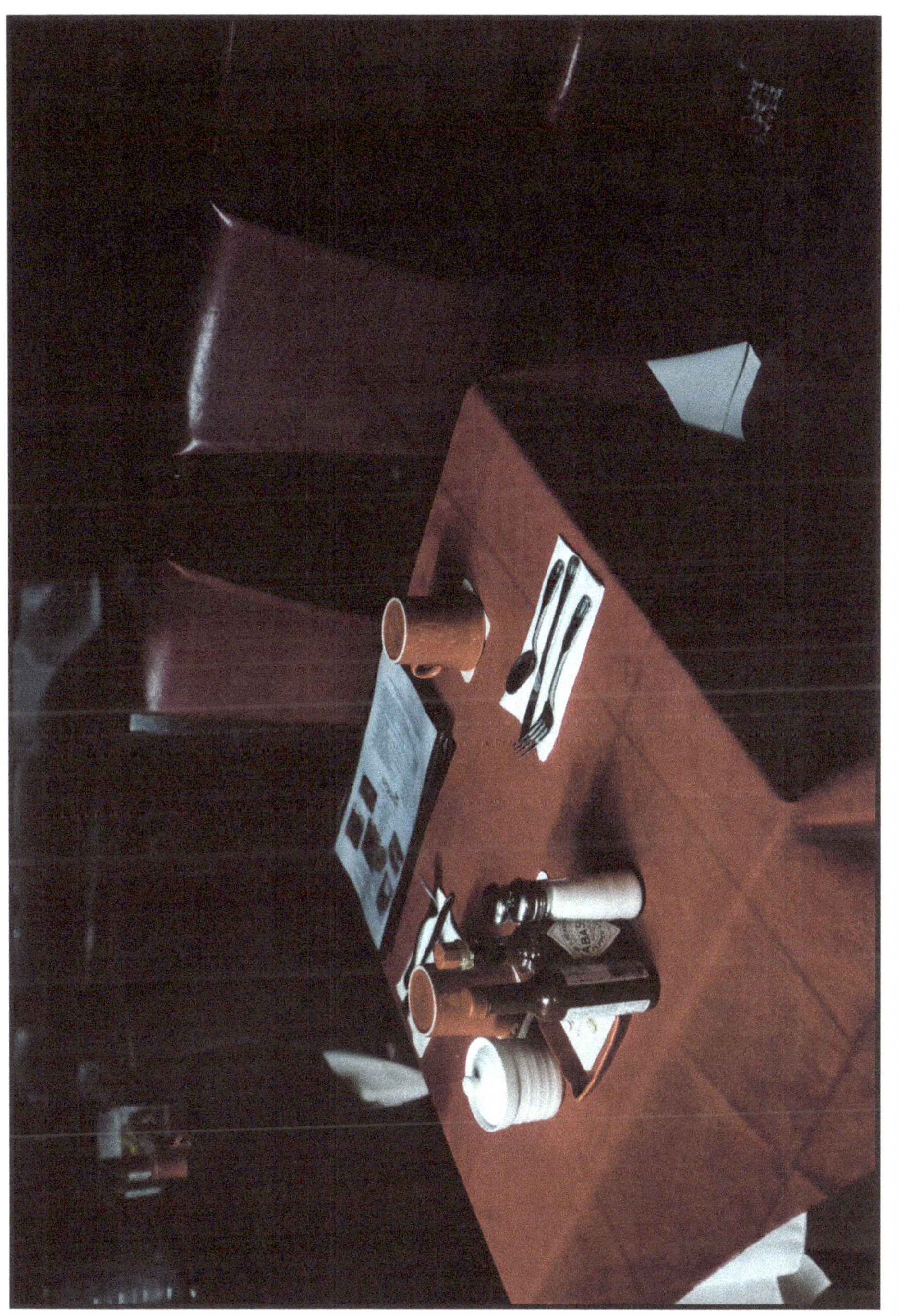

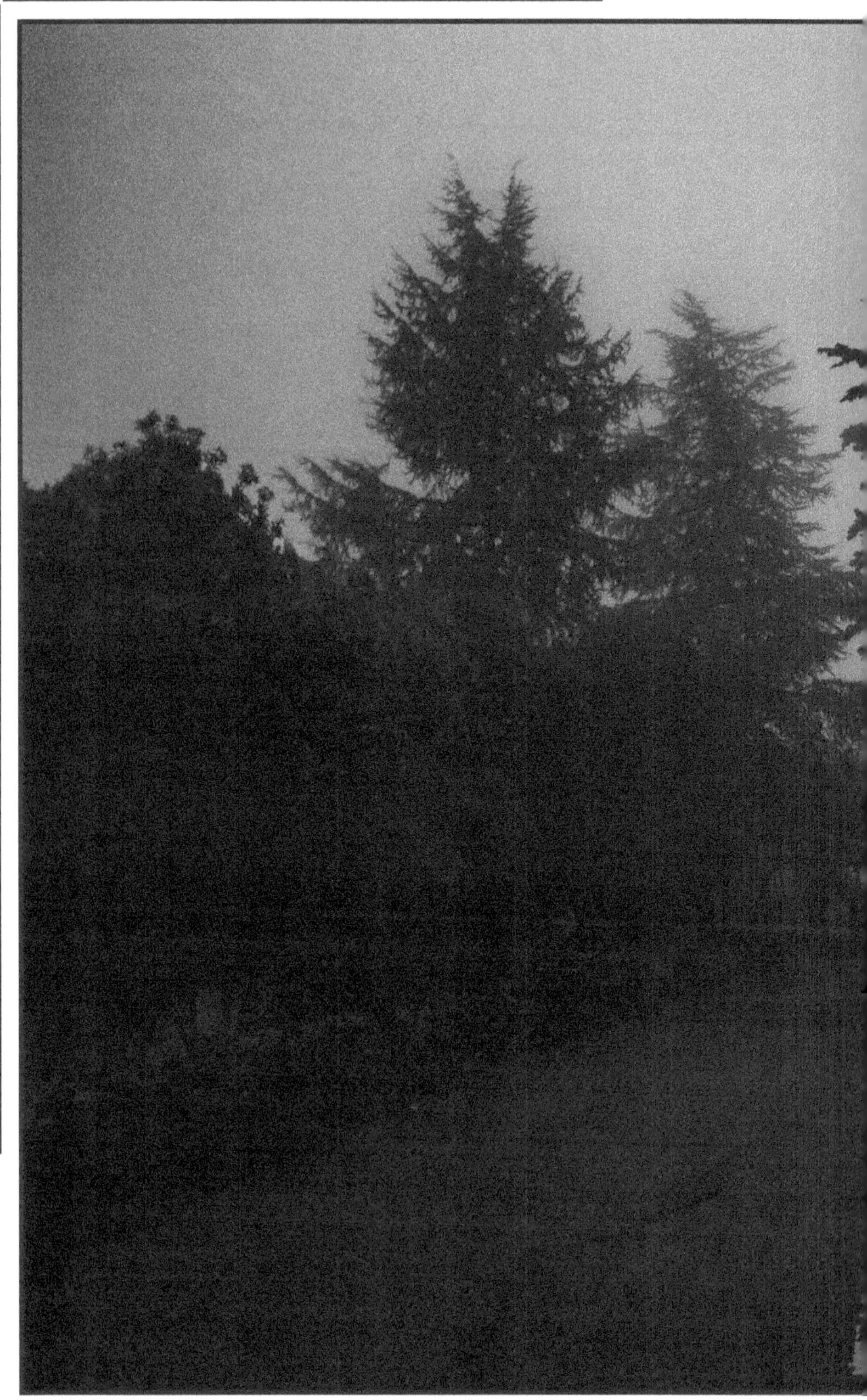

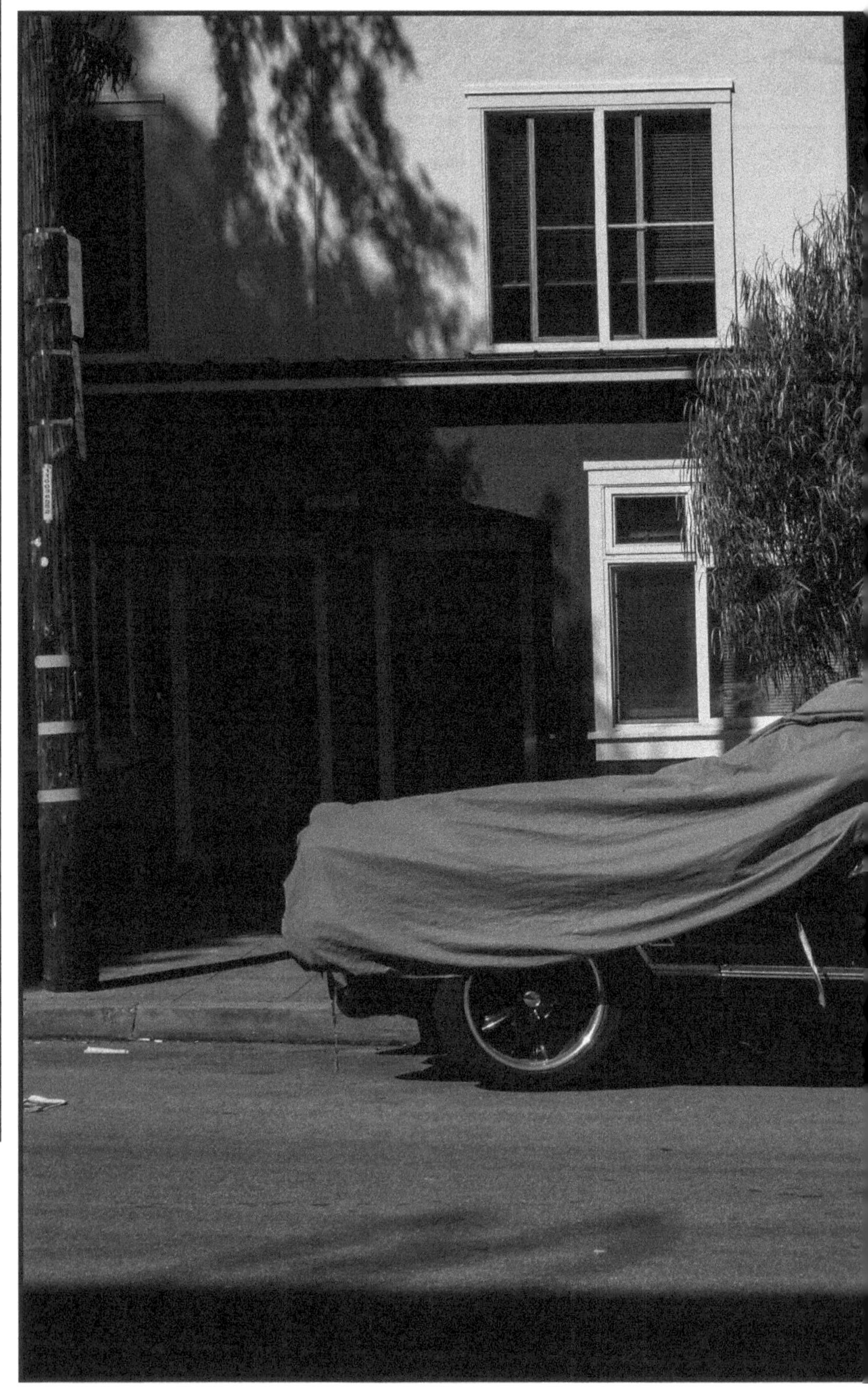

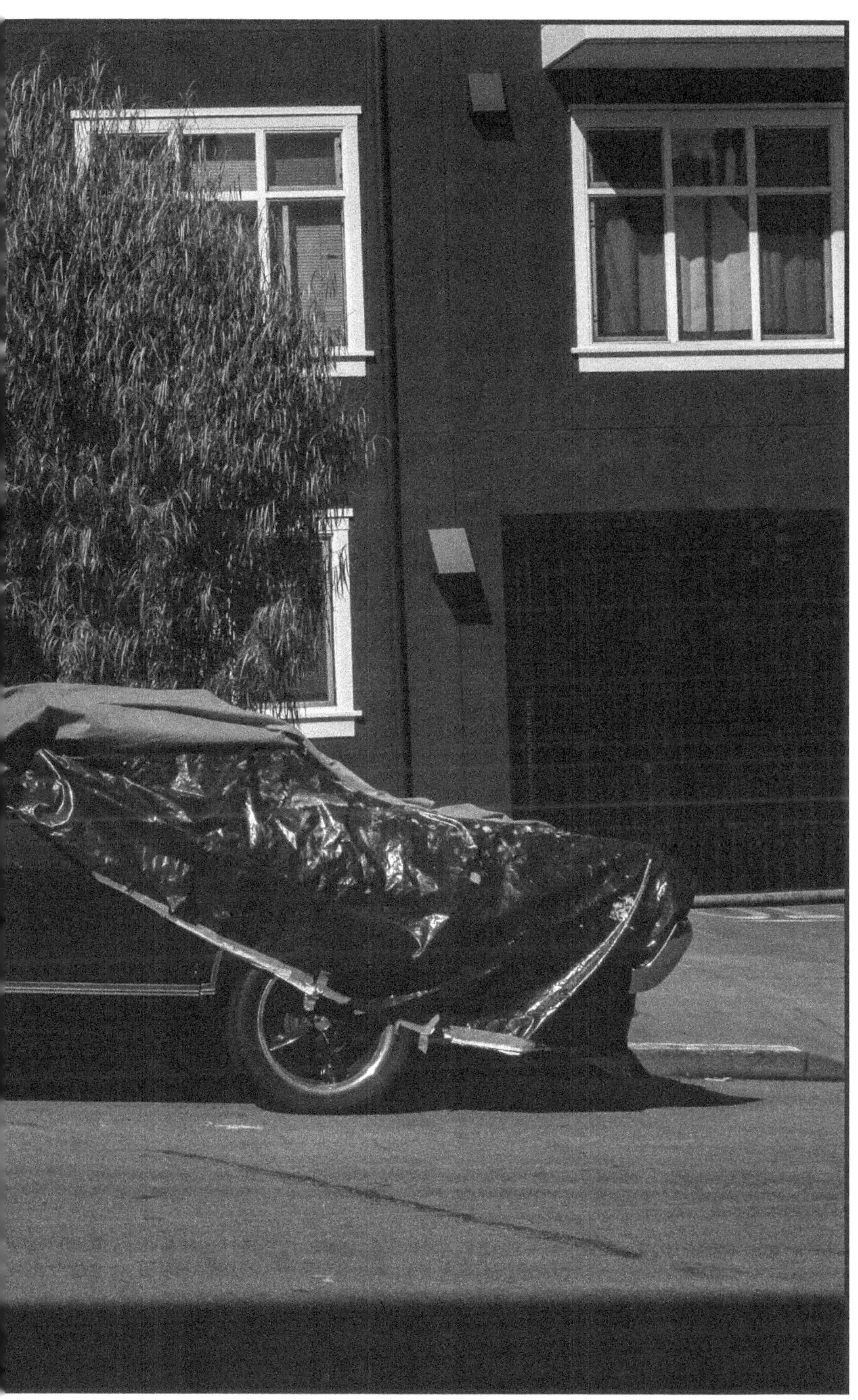

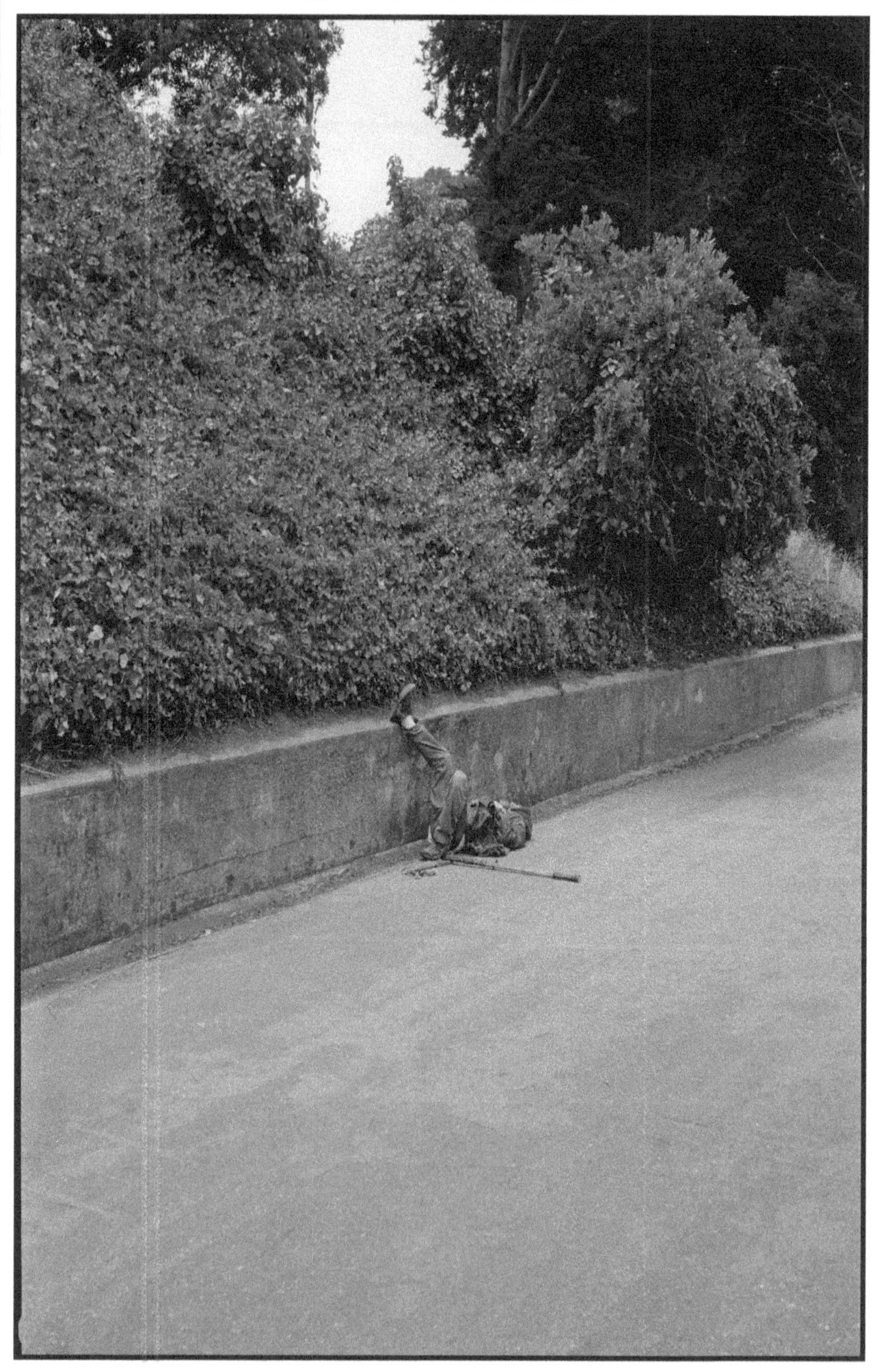

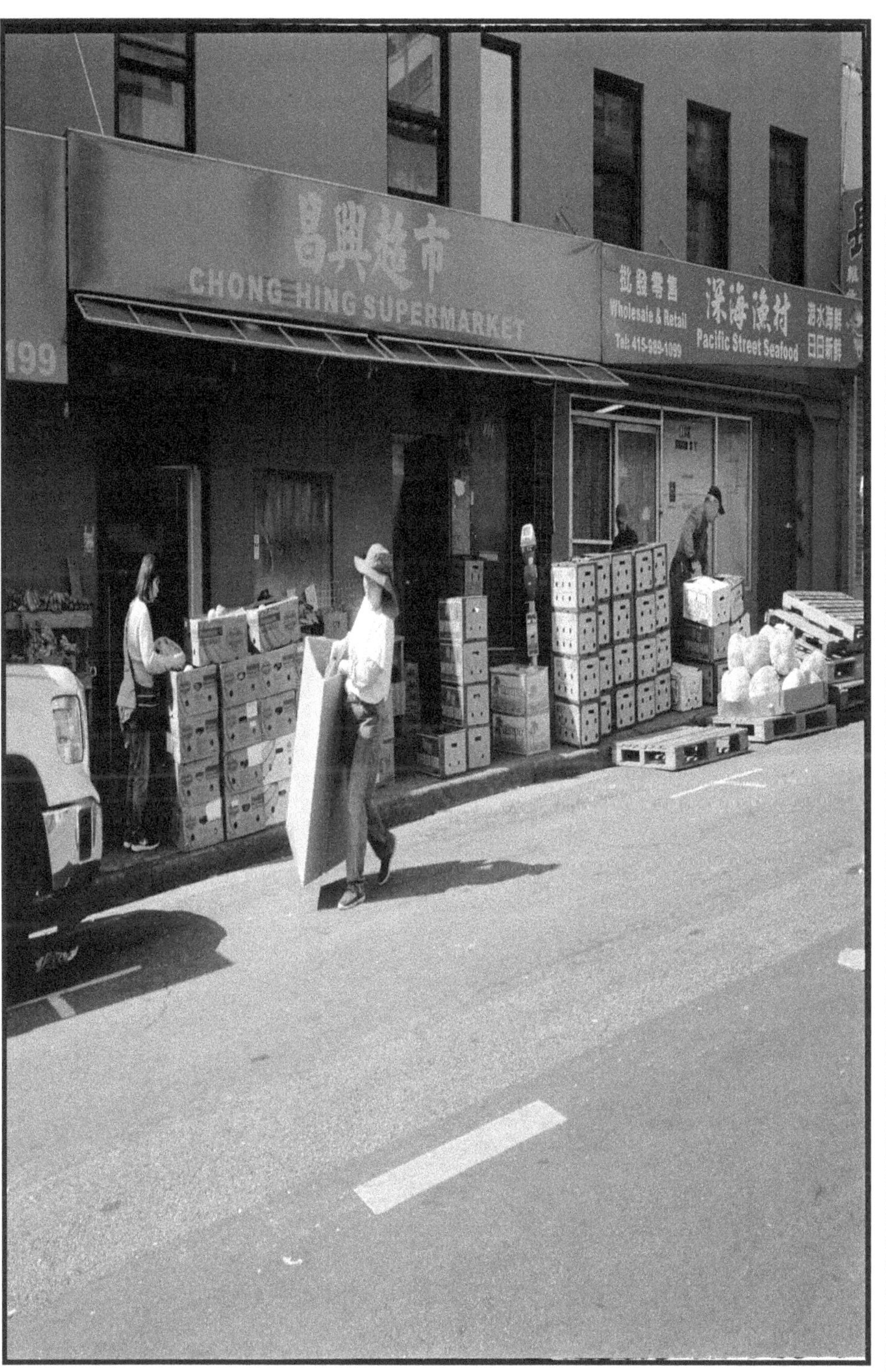
昌興超市
CHONG HING SUPERMARKET
199
批發零售
Wholesale & Retail
Tel: 415-989-1099
深海漁村
Pacific Street Seafood
深水海鮮
日日新鮮

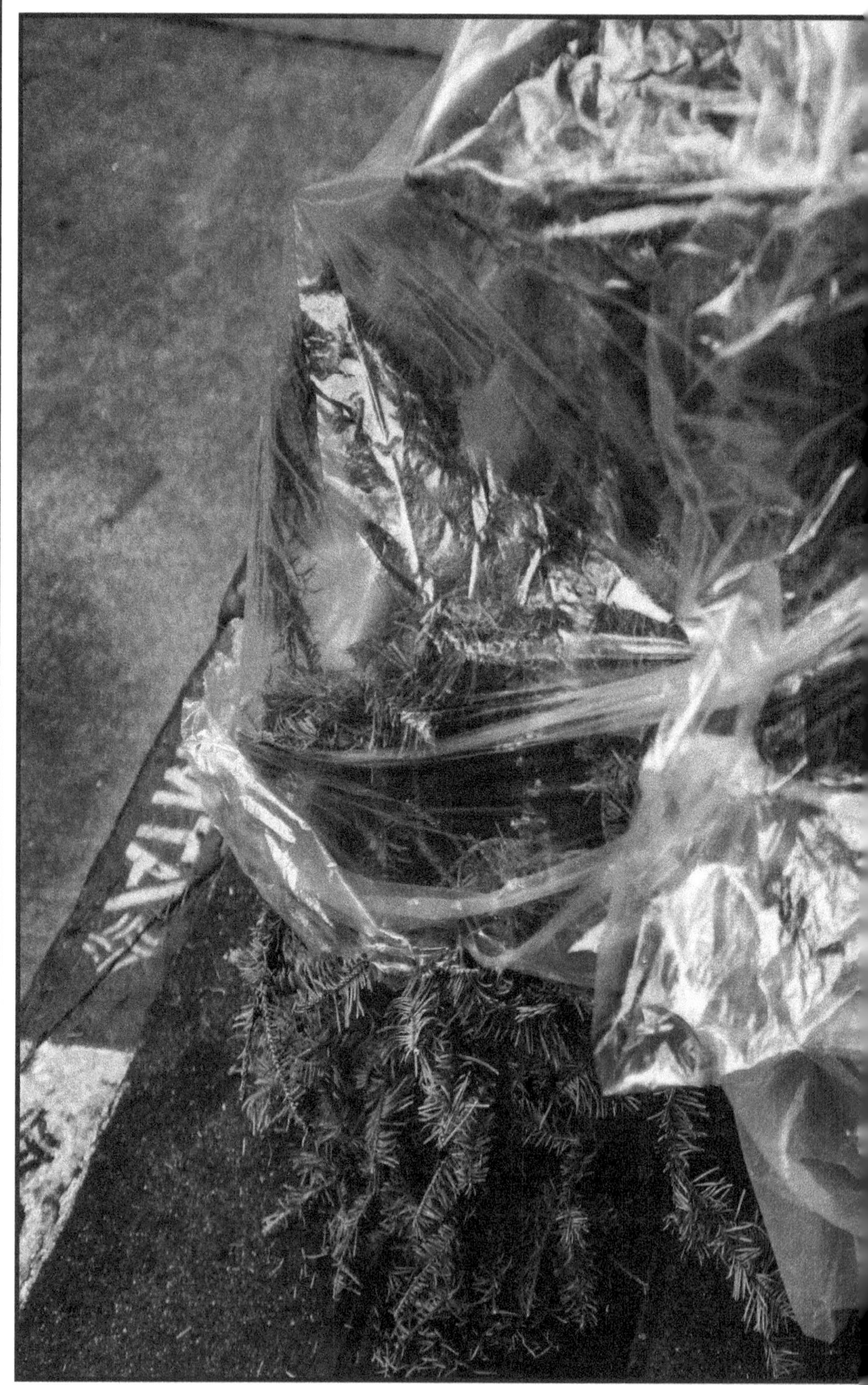

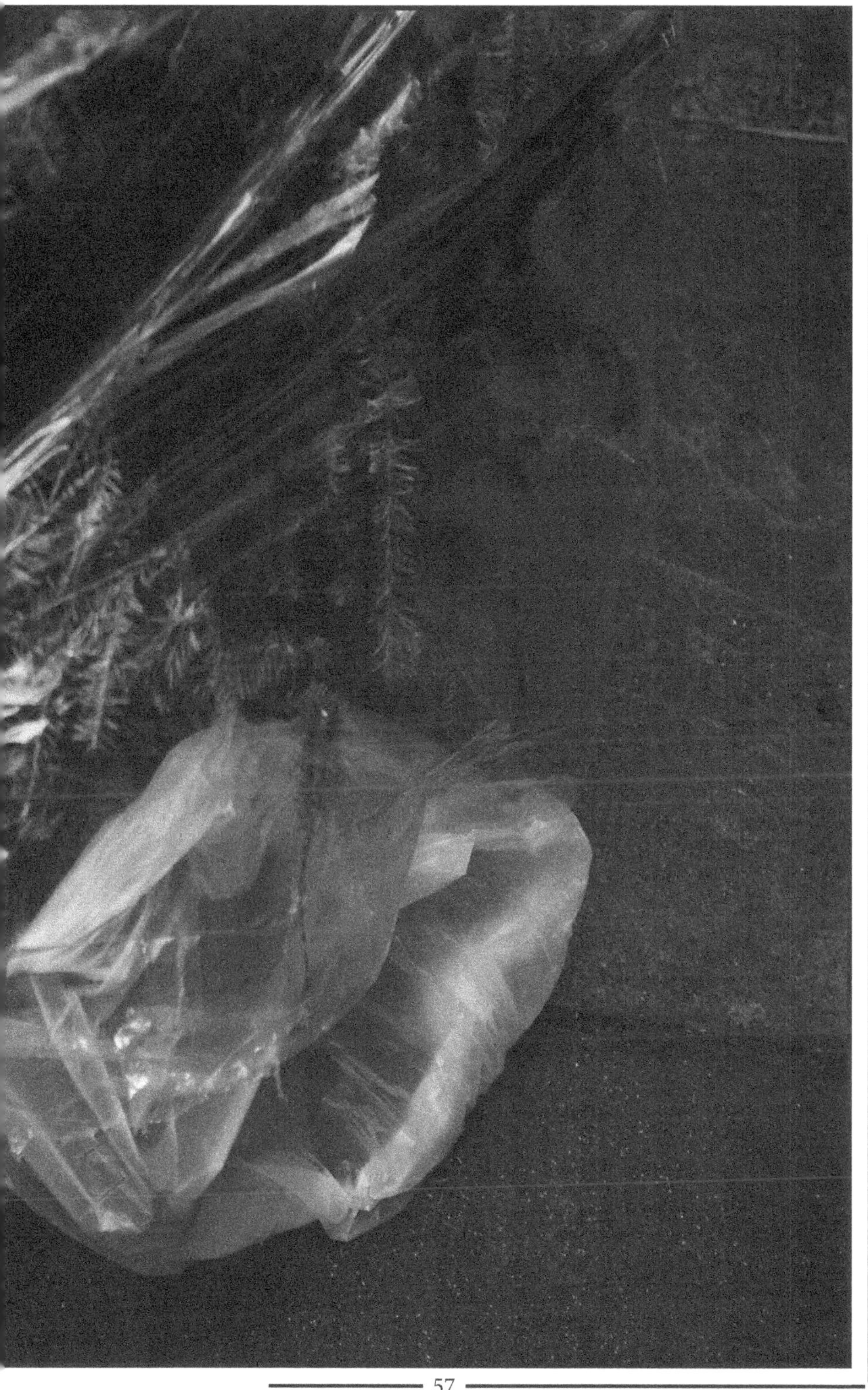

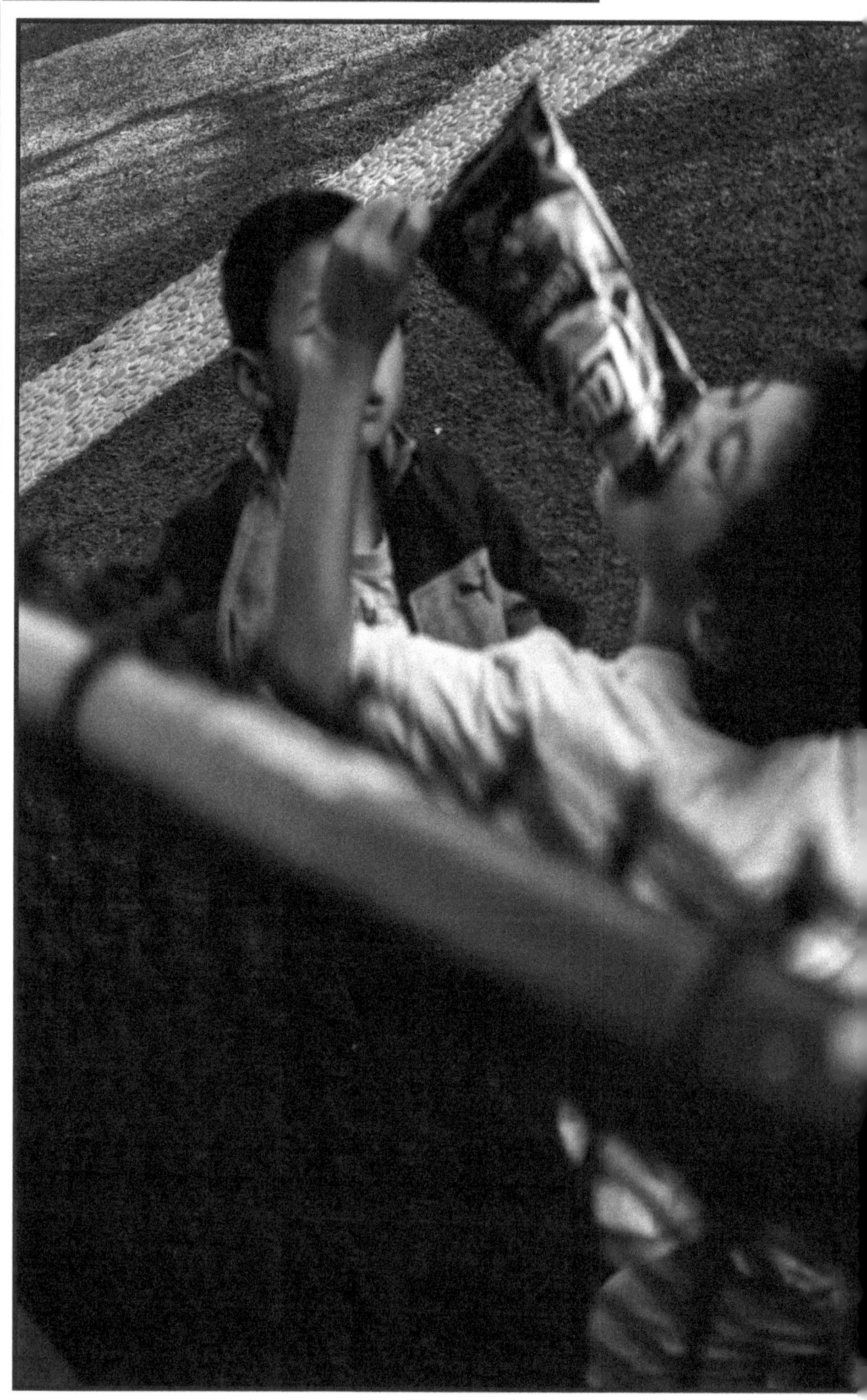

Pollard

Russell Helms

Within the walls of La Frappe, Pollard considered himself lucky to be part of the retinue of the Marquis Gavard who was his uncle. He did not have to work, save his studies with the philosopher Mouseman. Early morning and Pollard glanced himself in the mirror on the wall. His golden locks touched his shoulders, his face with a big smile pooching his rosy red lips. Pollard was slight in build, somewhat resembling a woman. He pulled on his velvet breeches and ruffled shirt of silk, headed to breakfast with the Marquis, the Marquis' wife, and the great philosopher Mouseman.

At table, there was a newspaper, which Mouseman was reading, decrying the violence of the Prussians but being sympathetic as it was in the nature of man to fight.

"All will be well, for nothing is as it should not be," said Mouseman.

Pollard gave vent to his thoughts. "Yes, you are right, as you have taught me. All men see fit to do as best they can given their circumstances." He munched an apple as the maid served tea.

Just then there was a booming knock at the door, as if it would break. The doorman of La Frappe had peeped through a window and seeing a passel of soldiers ran to the kitchen.

"The Prussians! Mon Dieu, the Prussians!" said the doorkeeper. He made for the kitchen door and fled through a garden.

The Marquis rose, trembling, and unbolted the door to be met by a corpulent corporal.

"You are spies for the enemy," said the corporal, his blue suit fringed with gold braid. "Stand aside!"

Into the manor of La Frappe entered a dozen soldiers, bayonets at the ready. The marquis' wife had come and stood behind her husband.

"Take them!" said the corporal.

Without ado, two soldiers advanced and fairly sliced the marquis and his wife into halves, their bleeding bodies tumbling to the floor. Just then Pollard and Mouseman appeared, fairly dejected at the sight before them. With haste they were bound and thrown upon horses and ridden to an encampment where they were beaten with cudgels and hung from a plane tree by their wrists.

Writhing just inches from the ground, Mouseman whispered to Pollard. "All is well. Had we been the marquis and his wife, we would be dead." His long face with a pretty moustache twitched.

Pollard thought. "Yes, you are right. Things could be much worse." He thought about his half-sister Moreline and wished to see her beauteous face once more. Alas, she had been visiting an aunt when the Prussians had arrived.

The next day, thoroughly stretched and dying of thirst, two horses with riders trotted into camp. Pollard could not believe his eyes. It was his dearest Moreline, whom he treasured. With his shoulders having become dislocated, he watched in horror as she was hung by the neck, her body then tossed aside. "They have killed dear Moreline," said Pollard.

"Yes, they have," said Mouseman wishing to tweak his moustache.

For six weeks, Pollard and Mouseman tramped, their hands bound behind their backs, eating but bread and drinking not enough water. Skirmishes with "the enemy" interrupted the long days. One fine day, the sun shining like the song of a lark, there was a great roar of cannon and rifle. Twas the Bulgarians!

In the melee, Pollard and Mouseman found themselves adrift and captured by the dirty Bulgarians. One among the group of their captors recognized the famous philosopher, and Mouseman was shot. Pollard watched with extreme anxiety, but soon took the Bulgarian uniform, and telling them of his knowledge gained while marching with the Prussians was put in charge of a light regiment.

Pollard excelled in his position, leading his men against all sorts of craven enemy including the Musselmen. He was always at the forefront of battle and led charges with cries of Zarezhdane! He oversaw the shooting of prisoners and quelled arguments over potato rations and horse meat, earning the charm of his men.

Sitting beside a roaring campfire, he mulled to himself. "All is as it should be. The world could not be more perfect. How I wish that poor Mouseman were with me." He then bethought the loss of his dear Moreline. He recalled her long black tresses, her massive bosom, and rutilant cheeks.

But, after a month, Pollard became bored and one night struck off for Vienna, which was nearby. With his little stash of gold, he rented a room. At noon, whilst shaving, there was a terrible ruckus in the streets and he besought to determine the cause. The potted meat workers were on strike!

Pollard ventured to the street to sate his curiosity. Lo and behold, he recognized his precious Moreline brandishing a pike, leading the uproarious crowd of potted meat workers. He fought his way to the fore, receiving a blow to the head, and called out.

"Moreline! You are saved. But how is it so? I saw you hanged by the Prussians!"

Moreline embraced him, being careful not to expose her arms. "Yes, tis I. The rope was poorly fashioned, and I could still breathe. I waited for the Prussian departure and took myself straightway to Dresden and thence to Vienna. Here, I have found purpose, but I do miss La Frappe and poor mother and father."

"Alas," said Pollard, "It is well as the great Mouseman would say. For how could I have met you here had not your parents been killed and you had been hanged?"

"Tis true," said Moreline, "but I must needs continue this day with my task. Meet me at the Hotel Gran at six." And with that she was off, brandishing her pike.

Poor Pollard watched as she was carried away with her work. She was soon arrested and thrown into gallows, but Pollard had no way of knowing, and he was vexed when he could not find her. Thinking that she must have fled to some other town in search of another cause, for she was energetic and of a singular mind, Pollard racked his brains. Knowing not what to do, he betook by foot a peregrination, which landed him in Italy in the quaint town of Vino Verde.

By this time, he was scarce of money, and betook a job making hard sausages. His hands covered with blood and fat, he wondered at his life and found that all was as it should be and hoped for the best. Having made a trifle, but enough upon which to travel, he embarked yet again soon arriving at the coast of the Adriatic.

Speaking not the language, he accidentally called a large man in a grog house by an untoward name and was beaten to within an inch of his life. Lying in a gutter, refuse flowing around him, he looked up at the stars wishing to see once again his beloved Moreline. His face battered by many blows, he could only smile, remembering the great Mouseman and knew that he would have to take courage and continue on.

At a small seaside port, Pollard hired on as a sailor, sharing a room with ten men swinging in their hammocks. They spoke not his language, and he was very careful in choosing his words. The crew struck him as disagreeable, unknowing of the meaning of life, and he departed their company in Albania. He had by this time, from much toil and labor, become a thin man. His first task was to visit a barber where his golden locks were trimmed and powdered.

He found lodging in a rooming house and upon entering the dining chamber there was amazed. His heart leapt into his throat, for behind the bar, sure enough, was the blessed Mouseman, pouring out wine from huge jugs. Pollard was besought with glee and agitation.

Mouseman seemed subdued. "Yes, it is I. The bullets did not kill me. I have done what is best in life and have taken what is given me."

Pollard sat upon a hard wooden stool, the perfume of his locks in his nose, but there was also the smell of heavy foods fried in grease.

"Oh, how happy I am," said Pollard. "You are surely right when you observe that all things happen according to plan. For if you had not been shot I would not have met you here. What a joy to see your ideas in motion!"

The great philosopher seemed unmoved by this rhetoric that was his.

"Yes, what is shall be and always. Listen, my lad, I have a favor to ask. I have a nephew who lives in the dread mountains of Transylvania. He is very rich and would gladly see to it that we were returned to the blessed La Frappe. I wish to spend my last days there."

Without a hitch, Pollard agreed, and buying a worn map took foot to his new journey. Four weeks of travel brought him into the mountains and with inquiry he located the castle of the Count Morass. After introductions, he belied the plans of Mouseman and was delighted to find the Count agreeable. The Count was dressed in black with a red rose in his long beard and red epaulettes upon his shoulders. He was a handsome man, but white as snow, and his eyes seemed like bricks of coal.

That night, as Pollard lay sleeping in a large bed of goose down, the Count entered his room and began sucking at his neck. Pollard felt the fangs bite his flesh and gave a mighty struggle soon running from the castle and losing himself in the dark moonlit woods.

"Mon Dieu!" was all he could muster.

Still with his mind on Moreline, and forgetting the wishes of Mouseman, Pollard set forth to the coast once again and boarded a ship headed for South America. As this seemed proper, Pollard, hoping for the best, toiled away at sail and net during the long journey. Alas, though, there was a mutiny passing by the Canary Islands. The inmates, as they were, caused much bloodshed, but were soon put down with musket and knife and thrown overboard. This much frightened Pollard, and he had to beg for his life in front of the mangy captain, swearing he had no involvement. He was beaten nonetheless and developed a limp as a result. But was he not alive?

The ship regained its course to French Guiana, and Pollard rejoiced that he would be among the company of his countrymen. The ship landed with strict orders that all were to return by nightfall under threat of death. Pollard found the natives quite cheerful amid their destitute poverty and took upon himself a journey into the interior to discover the cause of this happiness.

After three days walking, his shoes flopping about his feet, he found himself at a small stream and thus began to drink. Of a sudden was a piercing pain in his side, and he found an arrow there deeply embedded. He fell into the stream and was attacked by some ravenous fish but was pulled from the water bleeding. The strange little brown men bound him and hung him from a pole, carrying him like a dead pig to their village where were open-air huts leaking the smoke of cookfires.

Tied to a bujumka tree, Pollard wondered at his condition, but recalled the memes of his counselor the great philosopher Mouseman and parlayed himself into a state of mental wellness. On the third day, he was given the meat of a monkey to eat and felt some better but was alarmed by the building of a rather large fire and roasting spit. He was going to be cooked!

But first, a man masked in black, completely naked except for rude swashes of ochre upon his body, brought to Pollard a brew in a wooden bowl. As instructed, Pollard drank the brew, which tasted like sour wine mixed with dirt. All around him had gathered the villagers, watching in expectation. Within minutes, Pollard began to wretch and vomit, soiling himself. Great rainbows of color vibrating with electricity filled his brain. He knew not where he was and a great peace enveloped him, a smile coming to his lips.

This reaction pleased the villagers mightily, and he was unbound from the tree, whereupon he made haste to return to the coast, but disoriented went further into the jungle. Having discovered his error upon the third day, he decided that it was meant to be and pressed forward. Within six weeks, he had passed into Mexico and learned to answer of all that asked that he was looking for God, which brought nods of appreciation.

He passed through Texas, being dragged behind a bull for eating wild mushrooms, strayed south into Louisiana, being tarred and feathered for stealing sugar cane, found himself in the strange sounding Mississippi, where he took refuge with escaped slaves and ate cornbread mixed with syrup, ventured into Alabama where he was bitten by a rattlesnake, and then tired and unable to continue farther sank into the middle of a dirt road that passed through the small town of Whitesburg, Tennessee.

An old soldier rescued him from the road and secreted him in a small bunkhouse shared by three others. Having learned some English, Pollard spoke with his mates, learning of the town and its environs. He spoke to them of his beloved Mouseman and forthwith prodded them with his knowledge of good will to all should the occasion arise. He also spoke of the lovely Moreline, wounded by thoughts of her adrift in the world.

On his fourth day, Pollard ventured out and pushed into one of the many bars. Lo and behold twas Moreline serving drinks, whiskey and bourbon. He fell to his knees, covering her hands with kisses before taking a long look at her face and figure. Her long black hair had become gray and seemed chopped at the shoulders. Her hourglass figure had reversed itself, her chest seeming flat and her waist like that of a barrel. Stunned, but hoping for the best, he acquiesced himself to this new Moreline, considering it his duty to take what came his way. He had loved her before and was it not right to love her still?

His many kisses upon her hands had not gone unnoticed, and a large beef-steak of a man took exception.

"Who are ye, messing with my woman?" said the tall man with the chest of a horse.

"Oh, Bart, please. He is an old friend," said Moreline in perfect English.

Pollard rose from his knees, his chin meeting his foe's chest. "It is well that you are Moreline's lover, for it could not be otherwise. However, I love her and she must be mine."

At that, Bart grabbed Pollard's locks and plunged his mighty fist into Pollard's face, breaking his nose. Pollard reeled and fell back to his knees, the stars of heaven playing before his eyes. He saw a leg before him and withdrawing a knife plunged it into the flesh. But alas, he had stabbed another, the son of the constable.

Pollard awoke, his chin smarting and two teeth missing, inside a crude jail cell, iron bars in front and heavy brick around. He recalled the events and wished for something to eat. He spoke aloud, calling for his jailer, wishing that his poor Mouseman would appear to save him from this trouble, for he would find a way to make everything right.

On the third day, at midnight, as Pollard lay on his back counting the cracks in the ceiling, there was a mighty explosion. Pollard was thrown to floor, covered with brick and mortar.

"Come quick!" and it was Moreline who had set off the dynamite.

"Mon Dieu!" said Pollard, crawling through the jagged hole.

On two horses, they galloped into the night, a full moon lighting the way. After some twenty leagues, the horses fagged and wet, the pair stopped whereupon Pollard descried his love for her. They bedded in the pine straw and not having blankets slept close to one another, Pollard trembling with delight at her womanly smell.

"All is well and good night, my dear," said Pollard, squeezing Moreline's porcine shoulder.

"Yes, we shall find our way home and be married," said Moreline.

Within four weeks, they had reached Boston and selling the horses took a

room together. For two days they slept. In the next room was staying a minor bank-
er saving his pennies on lodging. In the middle of the night, he was robbed of three
hundred dollars by a man with golden hair and Pollard was arrested as the perpetrator.
Moreline begged his release, watching as he was carried away to gaol.

Pollard chalked up his situation to destiny, telling himself that nothing could
be otherwise and that all would be well. He was found guilty of theft, whipped, and set
aboard a frigate with thirty other prisoners to be deported back to their homelands.

The ship stopped first at Brighton and continued for Le Havre, where he was
disgorged less than forty leagues from his precious manor of La Frappe just outside of
Paris. He was received by the authorities with a sneer, but they soon realized he was
of the second estate and released him, for the jails were crowded anyway. Walking,
and without a sous to his name, Pollard made his way southwest, stopping briefly in
Bourneville to beg some alms from the parish priest. With a single louis in the pocket of
his tattered breeches and with a light snow he continued on now barefoot and bedrag-
gled.

On the outskirts of Paris, Pollard was attacked by a large Newfoundland and
bitten through the left arm. Bleeding, and with just an hour's walk to go, he refused the
attentions of an old woman, and soon came to the magnificent gate of La Frappe, but
it was locked with a heavy chain. Pollard picked up a stone and beat upon the gate as
if for air and lo the old doorman came rushing from within, followed by the maid. The
lock was undone, and Pollard collapsed to his knees as he kissed the ground. There was
a woman's voice he recognized, and he looked up.

"My dearest, Pollard!" The woman threw her fat arms around him.

"Moreline?" said Pollard.

He stood, and she squeezed him. He quickly assayed the conundrum, smiled,
and resolved that all was as it should be.

A Place for You

Jessamyn Wolff

In the home goods section of TJ Maxx
I waste time looking at fake succulents,
bending their sticky but pretty leaves
in all directions. Across the aisle, rows
of decorative glass jars line the shelves.
A large one stands out, flowers painted
at its bottom shine pink in the fluorescent
light. As I hold it, kids and their moms
push red carts around me, employees
hurry by with loops full of shrill keys.
I determine that, yes, all I have left of you
will fit in this glass jar—pictures of you
at the piano, the plastic Pokémon won
in a bet, your charcoal drawings if I fold
them. The woman working the counter
compliments my choice as she wraps it
in pale, crinkling paper—*this'd be great
for a candle, it really catches the light.*
Outside, the sun's been smeared with
silver clouds. I walk home underneath
its haze, crying so hard I think my eyes
will burst and fall like rain at my feet.

Tonight Your Ghost

Emily Kingery

Tonight your ghost will ask my ghost
Who put these bodies between us?
--Metric, "Calculation Theme"

We enter the cemetery to touch
the illegible names on stones,

quiet and damp to our skin
as cellars, even now, when

the brittle August grass
breaks under us like cereal.

Oak branches snap as squirrels
leap in fright, in play; teenagers

swerve their parents' cars to the edges
where there are no plots.

We guess they stash drugs in the glove boxes,
undress each other, and we are right

without knowing if we are.
Decades have slipped from our lives

since we did the same, though it's wrong
to say we are in mourning, even if

we are. I have imagined the two
of your exes who died by suicide

are the air wicking away our sweat,
are the birds the size of gargoyles

calling out for each other in the
voices of cats. *That says something*

about us, you say, but you don't say
what I want. When high beams swoop

68

our path, they light animals preying
on each other. We feel afraid

of ourselves. We are never so ready
to run or to maul a pitiful body down

to bone, never ready. I know
what I want. I want what animals want

when they are threatened, when the light
has been dissolved. I am willing your mouth

to say, *We will*, to complete the sentence
with flesh, with impulse, with car windows

clouded with breath instead of weather.
The insects are violent in our ears.

You say if the gates are shut when we leave,
we will go around them, like ghosts.

Take a mattress. Put it in our woods.

Art by Victoria Parker
Poetry by Kristin Withers

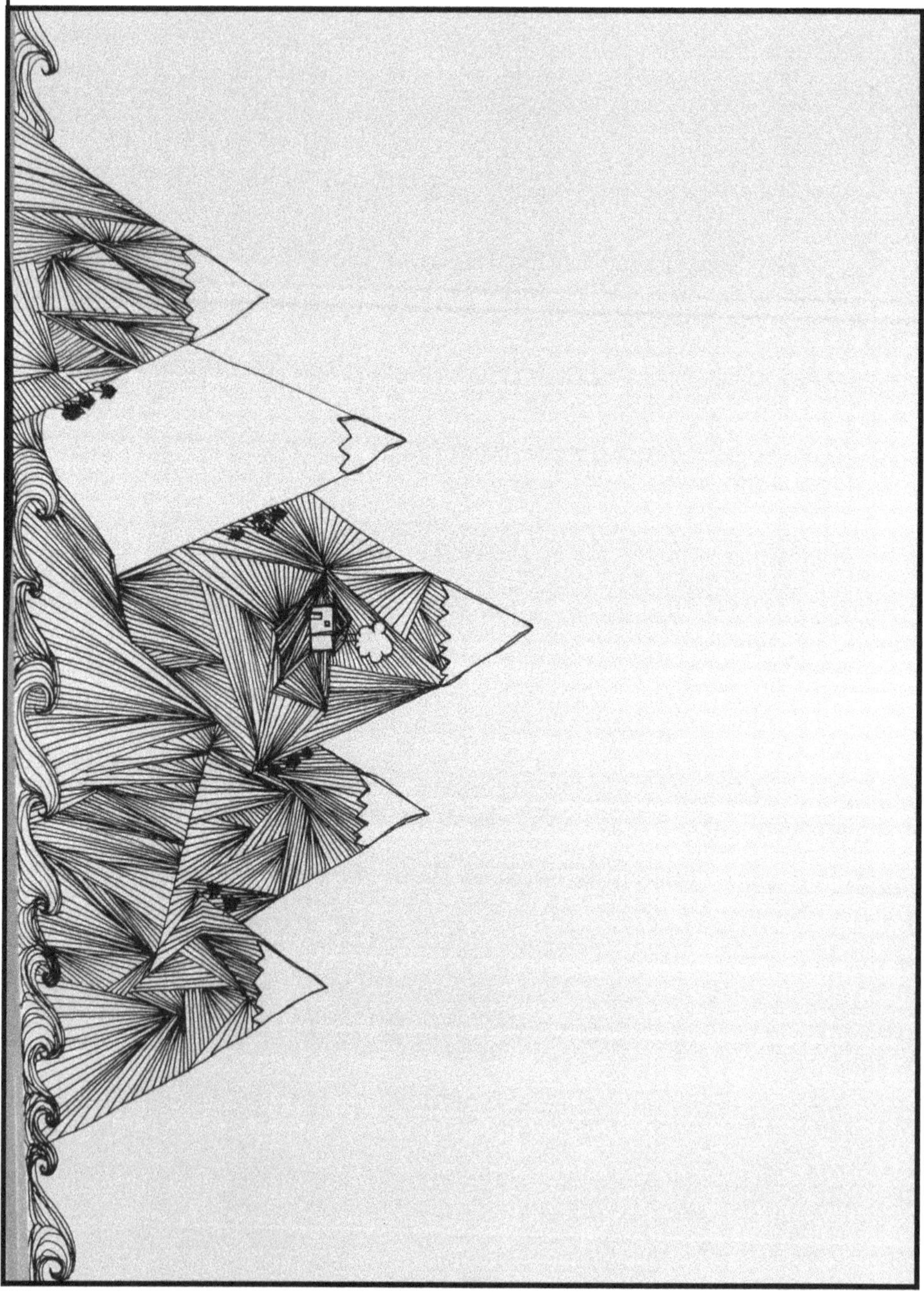

how it is you have found yourself within
        me; found you out – antlers scuttling raw
        around the lake,

        again & again, a determination
found in my pacing, so that
        looming in the floral spores before their teething

churned bit by bit & lived in – I have
been in you,
        one referent & oscillating twilight

of the symmetries we are authors
        nacreous not recreant
the first folders of wedding dress & sewists

of mudded foul & too,
        the congenital dowry
an exercise in every

        djinn in fugue & moving
root; confession – even in turning
from me – when I was both

contractual & of plasticity – being both
        there and feeling,
        our imbued room (trespassed)

as I returned —
        sanguine & slept in
        having unbecome you & been menstruous

I used my hands & still the sea
rich in silver chevron & no smell
        to remember, how it would no longer reveal itself

        (but these disobedient
        salivas —showing themselves & collating)
but mistook the cadence of a quest for a guest

In Order Of Appearance:

Patricia Thrushart has published two books, Little Girl Against The Wall, and Yin and Yang. Her work appears regularly in The Watershed Journal, a regional literary magazine of Northwestern Pennsylvania, and on the websites Dark Horse Appalachia and North/South Appalachia. Her poems have been published in Tiny Seed, The Brookville Mirror, Clarion University's Tobeco, The Avocet, Still Point Arts Quarterly, The Pittsburgh Post Gazette, The Indiana Gazette, Feminine Collective and The Pennsylvania Poetry Society's Magazine PENNESSENCE. She is an active member of the local writers' community, presenting workshop sessions and participating in live poetry readings.
www.patriciathrushart.com

Desiree Dufresne is interested in exploring the many facets of life through the lenses of curiosity, critique, wonder, and spontaneity. Her abstractions of the experiences of women, queer people, and the human condition itself seek to find affirmation of life in the midst of sadness and anxiety. She has a reverence for art of all kinds, and is a voracious consumer of visual art, film, written works, and performance art. She lets herself soak in the genius of other artists and refracts her inspirations through her own unique perspective. The self-taught artist works mostly with acrylic and oil paint, but also likes to play with gouache and watercolor here and there. Her unique sense of texture and composition brings the viewer into another world of perception wherein colors and shapes tell a story that is meant to be creatively interpreted. She loves working with different paint media and exploring the strengths and challenges of each one. Her application is confident, irreverent, and at times absurd, but every line, scribble, distorted shape, and unusual color is applied with studied intent. Desiree works as a teacher in Los Angeles, CA and has received two degrees in History. She has been accepted to the MFA in Fine Arts program at the admired OTIS College of Art and Design, and plans to begin classwork next year. Her artwork is included in several private art collections throughout the Untied States. She has also created many commissioned works of art.

Kent Weigle is an admirer of nature, especially of birds. He earned his MFA from the Rainier Writing Workshop, and is a contributing editor for Palaver out of the University of North Carolina at Wilmington's Graduate Liberal Studies program. He currently lives haphazardly in Boston.

Nathaniel Hughes is a father, librarian, and writer who lives with his wife, son, and two black cats (one of whom is trans) in Kansas City. He thinks adults should stop underestimating youth and instead try to work with them to fix all this shit we have going on. Nathaniel compiled a decades worth of prose, poetry, and two letters into a compilation narrative about his life and struggles with addiction, relationships, mental health, and recovery. It is titled Three Years This August. Nathaniel is nearly three years sober. He wants people to be more kind.

Brazilian author Beatriz Seelaender has had essays published by websites such as The Collapsar and The Manifest-Station, and her short stories can be found in Psychopomp Lit Mag, The Gateway Review and others. Her story "A Kidney Caught in Quicksand", published by Grub Street in 2017, earned recognition from the Columbia Scholastic Press Association in the categories of experimental fiction and humor writing. In 2019, Seelaender won Hidden River Arts' Sandy Run Novella Award.
You can check out her weekly column at Maudlin House (dot net).

Nikita Petrov was born in 1986 in Barnaul (Siberia, Russia). In 2010 graduated from The Altai State Technical University The Architecture and Design Institute. Since 2012 has been living and working in St.Petersburg (Russia).

Mandy graduated from Pacific Lutheran University in August of 2012. Her fiction has appeared in Whitefish Review Literary Journal and 100 Word Story.
She lives in Corvallis, Oregon. She loves rain and pizza in no particular order.

Felice Arenas was a writer and editor for Netflix and interviewed filmmakers and musicians for HuffPost before earning her MFA from New York University, where she taught and was a Global Research Initiatives fellow. Born and raised in Chicago, she has lived in Los Angeles, New York City, Brooklyn, and Shanghai.

Michael Kreger is a Philadelphia native who attended Temple University graduating with a degree in English Literature and Philosophy. He has been teaching in public schools for the past eleven years. Most recently, Michael was the principal at a charter school in Denver, Colorado where he has resided with his partner for the past six years. Michael is interested in the intersection of the artificial and the natural and how the incongruent nature of those two powerful forces shape our lives on a daily basis. Currently, Michael is residing Mexico City working on his first full length manuscript of poems.

Laura Mota is a Brazilian writer and portrait photographer based in Montreal. Her poetry has appeared in Portal Magazine and Dreamers Magazine. A collection of her poems in Portuguese, Pseudocasos, was published in 2018.

Paris Weslyn is the return of Spring, creeping forth to cast out the darkness of Winter. Residing in Portland, Oregon, she is a Black woman refreshed, reborn, and blossoming, whose purpose is to respond to existence with awe and wonder.

ky li is a folk poet in Louisville, Kentucky whose work has appeared in Brittle Star, The Oddville Press, The Ibis Head Review, West Trade Review, and the books Six Voices and Six Voices Two, published in 2017 and 2019 by Blackthorn Press. ky's poem, "A Physicist Explains Irregular Escapement," appears in Issue 44/June 2019 of Brittle Star and two other poems will appear in the 2019 fall/winter issue of Word Fountain. ky completed a MA in creative writing/poetry in the summer of 2018.

Ami J. Sanghvi is a 25-year-old, female, Indian-American, queer writer, photographer, activist, and mixed martial artist. At this time, she's self-published four poetry books: Amaranthine (2018), Devolution (2019), Armageddon (2019), and Silk & Cigars (2019), and is also pursuing her M.F.A. in Creative Writing at the California Institute of the Arts. Her essay, "Aladdin," is scheduled to be published by Awakenings (The Nightingale) (publishing date: November 21, 2019), and her poetic-prose piece, "The Cycle of Embers," by The Showbear Family Circus (publishing date: TBA).

M. SHAYNE BELL received a Creative Writing Fellowship from the National Endowment for the Arts (1991). His poem, "One Hundred Years of Russian Revolution," was a finalist for the Rhysling Award (1989). His poetry has been published in The Fibonacci Review, The Ghazal Page, Shot Glass Journal, Typishly, Dialogue, Sunstone, Amazing Stories, Asimov's, etc. His haiku have been published in Modern Haiku, The Heron's Nest, Tinywords, Sunstone, and Mainichi Japan.

Bell also publishes science fiction and fantasy. His story "Mrs. Lincoln's China" was a finalist for the Hugo Award (1995). His story "The Pagodas of Ciboure" was a finalist for the Nebula Award (2002). He received a first place Writers of the Future award (1990) for his story "Jacob's Ladder." His works include the novel Nicoji, the anthology Washed by a Wave of Wind: Science Fiction from the Corridor (for which he received an Award for Editorial Excellence from the Association for Mormon Letters [1994]), and the story collection How We Play the Game in Salt Lake. His nearly 100 published stories have appeared in Asimov's, The Magazine of Fantasy and Science Fiction, Tomorrow, Analog, Amazing Stories, etc.; in The Year's Best Fantasy and Horror (2003); and in three editions (2000, 2001, 2004) of The Year's Best Science Fiction. He has written stories for both Star Wars and Star Trek. Bell holds Bachelor's (1982) and Master's (1985) degrees in English Literature from Brigham Young University. In 1993, Bell backpacked through Haleakala Volcano on Maui, from the summit to the sea, retracing an expedition Jack London went on in 1911. In 1996, Bell was part of an eight-day expedition to the summit of Kilimanjaro. Bell's long-time companion, Drew Staffanson (a foreign correspondent who had been stationed at various posts in the Middle East), died in 2002. Bell grew up on a ranch outside of Rexburg, Idaho (USA); he and his six cats live in Rexburg. Bell's works in progress include A Year for Music, an autobiography told through encounters with music (see www.year4music.com); Apple Blossoms Falling, a book-length collection of original haiku; and Salt Lake in Tulips, Bell's decade's-worth of photographs of that city's spring flowers.

Patrick is a rising senior at Northview High School. He is an avid writer and artist always dedicated to searching out new voices. He has attended the Kenyon Review Young Writers workshop, been published by the American High School Poets, and excerpted in the New York Times. He is an avid defender of minority voices, his favorite television shows, and the Oxford comma.

Valyntina Grenier makes art on the side of life that insists, "Don't Shoot." Her poetry and visual art push the boundaries of representation and abstraction to create a vantage from which to view violence and prejudice. Her work has appeared or is forthcoming in, Lana Turner, JuxtaProse, Cathexis North West Press, Bat City Review, The Volta's Arroyo Chico and Spiral Orb. Her first chapbook Fever Dream/ Take Heart (a double) is due out January 2020 from Cathexis North West Press. Find her at valyntinagrenier.com or Insta @valyntinagrenier

Jerome Berglund graduated summa cum laude from the cinema-television production program at the University of Southern California, and has spent much of his career working in television and photography. He has had photographs (not the ones submitted here) published and awarded in local papers and recently staged an exhibition in the Twin Cities area which included a residency of several months at a local community center. The next show featuring his pictures, at the Pause Gallery in New York, is opening in late December.

Sasha Torchinsky is a queer artist born and raised in Vancouver, B.C. on the unceded traditional territory of the Musqueam, Squamish, and Tsleil-Waututh First Nations. Sasha is inspired by James Baldwin, reality television, and freaks everywhere.

yeting xiong: currently, study studio art as an MFA student at sfai

Russell Helms has had stories in Nowhere Magazine, Whitefish Review, Driftwood Press, Bewildering Stories, Drunken Boat, Sand, antiTHESIS, and other journals. He holds a lectureship in English at the University of Tennessee at Chattanooga. His novel, Fade, is forthcoming (2019) from Unsolicited Press.

Jessamyn Wolff is a poet and visual artist from West Michigan, currently working on her MFA at the University of Massachusetts Boston. Her work has recently appeared in Hanging Loose Press, Conception Arts Show, Storm of Blue Press, and the Boston Globe.

Emily Kingery is an Assistant Professor of English at St. Ambrose University in Davenport, Iowa, where she teaches courses in literature, writing, and linguistics. She serves on the board of directors at the Midwest Writing Center, a non-profit organization that supports writers in the Quad Cities community.

Visual artist Victoria Parker draws inspiration from dream worlds and contrasts in nature and urban environments. She collects odd vintage figurines and beach rocks and is currently saving up dryer lint with which she will make her brother a surprise doll. A native Seattleite, she has also lived in Kalamazoo, New York City and Okinawa, Japan. She lives in Seattle with her husband and two children.

Kristin Withers is a poet currently residing in the Pacific Northwest. She has been an industrial sewist, coffee roaster, bookseller, realty & teaching assistant. Kristin's disciplined in analytic philosophy, focusing particularly on epistemology & the metaphysics of consciousness. With initial publication at The Inquisitive Eater: New School Food, she is currently working on a gallery in liminal nocturne & a concept collection of autoscopic language poetry.

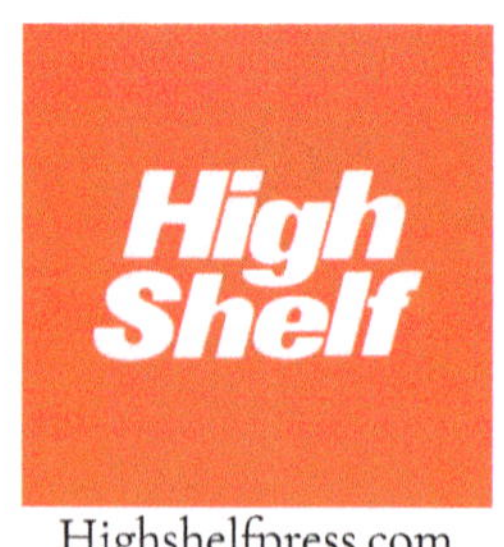

Highshelfpress.com